The Financial Effects of Inflation

NATIONAL BUREAU OF ECONOMIC RESEARCH

PHILLIP CAGAN

National Bureau of Economic Research and Columbia University

and

ROBERT E. LIPSEY

National Bureau of Economic Research and Queens College, CUNY

The Financial Effects of Inflation

National Bureau of Economic Research General Series No. 103

Published for the
NATIONAL BUREAU OF
ECONOMIC RESEARCH, INC.
by
BALLINGER PUBLISHING COMPANY
A Subsidiary of J. B. Lippincott Company
Cambridge, Mass.
1978

International Standard Book Number: 0-88410-486-9

Library of Congress Catalog Card Number: 78-13124

Printed in the United States of America

Library of Congress Cataloging in Publication Data

Cagan, Phillip.
    The financial effects of inflation.

    (General series — National Bureau of Economic Research ; 103)

    Bibliography: p.
    1. Inflation (Finance)—United States. 2. Finance—United States.
I. Lipsey, Robert E., joint author. II. National Bureau of Economic
Research. III. Title. IV. Series: National Bureau of Economic Re-
search. General series ; 103.
Gneral series ; 103.
HG538.C16   332.4'1   78-13124
ISBN 0-88410-486-9

RELATION OF THE DIRECTORS TO THE
WORK AND PUBLICATIONS OF THE
NATIONAL BUREAU OF ECONOMIC RESEARCH

1. The object of the National Bureau of Economic Research is to ascertain and to present to the public important economic facts and their interpretation in a scientific and impartial manner. The Board of Directors is charged with the responsibility of ensuring that the work of the National Bureau is carried on in strict conformity with this object.

2. The President of the National Bureau shall submit to the Board of Directors, or to its Executive Committee, for their formal adoption all specific proposals for research to be instituted.

3. No research report shall be published by the National Bureau until the President has sent each member of the Board a notice that a manuscript is recommended for publication and that in the President's opinion it is suitable for publication in accordance with the principles of the National Bureau. Such notification will include an abstract or summary of the manuscript's content and a response form for use by those Directors who desire a copy of the manuscript for review. Each manuscript shall contain a summary drawing attention to the nature and treatment of the problem studied, the character of the data and their utilization in the report, and the main conclusions reached.

4. For each manuscript so submitted, a special committee of the Directors (including Directors Emeriti) shall be appointed by majority agreement of the President and Vice Presidents (or by the Executive Committee in case of inability to decide on the part of the President and Vice Presidents), consisting of three Directors selected as nearly as may be one from each general division of the Board. The names of the special manuscript committee shall be stated to each Director when notice of the proposed publication is submitted to him. It shall be the duty of each member of the special manuscript committee to read the manuscript. If each member of the manuscript committee signifies his approval within thirty days of the transmittal of the manuscript, the report may be published. If at the end of that period any member of the manuscript committee withholds his approval, the President shall then notify each member of the Board, requesting approval or disapproval of publication, and thirty days additional shall be granted for this purpose. The manuscript shall then not be published unless at least a majority of the entire Board who shall have voted on the proposal within the time fixed for the receipt of votes shall have approved.

5. No manuscript may be published, though approved by each member of the special manuscript committee, until forty-five days have elapsed from the transmittal of the report in manuscript form. The interval is allowed for the receipt of any memorandum of dissent or reservation, together with a brief statement of his reasons, that any member may wish to express; and such memorandum of dissent or reservation shall be published with the manuscript if he so desires. Publication does not, however, imply that each member of the Board has read the manuscript, or that either members of the Board in general or the special committee have passed on its validity in every detail.

6. Publications of the National Bureau issued for informational purposes concerning the work of the Bureau and its staff, or issued to inform the public of activities of Bureau staff, and volumes issued as a result of various conferences involving the National Bureau shall contain a specific disclaimer noting that such publication has not passed through the normal review procedures required in this resolution. The Executive Committee of the Board is charged with review of all such publications from time to time to ensure that they do not take on the character of formal research reports of the National Bureau, requiring formal Board approval.

7. Unless otherwise determined by the Board or exempted by the terms of paragraph 6, a copy of this resolution shall be printed in each National Bureau publication.

(Resolution adopted October 25, 1926, as revised through September 30, 1974)

Contents

List of Figures

List of Tables

Foreword

In 1970 the National Bureau of Economic Research, with the support of a grant from the American Council of Life Insurance, undertook a major study of some of the important effects of inflation on financial markets. The present book began as a report of the overall project, but, as we brought in related work of others, the report grew into a survey of recent research on the financial effects of inflation. Although there are many aspects of inflation we do not attempt to deal with, we have endeavored, in drawing together the main results of the National Bureau's study and other work on the financial effects of inflation, to summarize what has been learned and what questions remain open.

We wish to acknowledge our indebtedness to the members of the study group, which included Jaspar H. Arnold, Phillip Cagan, Stanley Diller, Peter Fortune, John Lintner, Thomas Piper, Thomas Sargent, Lester Taylor, and Paul Wachtel. Publications resulting from this research are denoted in the bibliography by an asterisk. For extensive comments and suggestions on the present manuscript, we also wish to thank Solomon Fabricant, John Lintner, Kenneth Wright, the National Bureau's staff reading committee members, Stanley Fischer, Benjamin Friedman, and James Lothian; and the members of the Board of Directors reading committee: G. L. Bach, J. Wilson Newman, and Philip J. Sandmaier, Jr.

Finally, we are indebted to Raymond Goldsmith of the National Bureau, J. Heinrichs and John Musgrave of the Bureau of Economic Analysis, U.S. Department of Commerce, and Judith Ziobro of the Flow-of-Funds unit of the Federal Reserve Board for providing unpublished data; to Linda O'Connor for checking the tables; and to Muriel Moeller for preparing numerous versions of the manuscript.

Phillip Cagan
Robert E. Lipsey

The Financial Effects of Inflation

Chapter One

The Standard Theory up to the Mid-1960s

The rapid inflation since the mid-1960s has subjected financial markets to a series of unsettling disturbances.

Interest rates rose to high levels and fluctuated widely with swings in monetary policy. The purchasing power of outstanding securities depreciated, there were major changes in financial practices, and investors struggled to protect portfolios against inflation. Before the mid-1960s the United States had little experience with high inflation rates except in wartime. The events of the past decade have tested the standard theory of the effects of inflation developed over the years in economic literature, conforming to parts of the theory but also exhibiting important departures. This book discusses, first, the main propositions of the standard theory and, second, the nonconforming events since the mid-1960s which have led to modifications and extensions of the theory and have raised additional theoretical and empirical questions not yet answered.

A large part of the literature on the effects of inflation is devoted to analyzing the response of the economy to a depreciation in the purchasing power of money and financial assets. Inflation is viewed as imposing a tax on money balances and other assets fixed in dollar value and is often likened to an excise tax on a commodity.[1] Although exceptions can be found, the uniform approach of most of this literature warrants designation as the standard theory of the effects of inflation on the economy.[2] When inflation escalated in the mid-1960s, this theory provided the only organized set of ideas on the subject applicable to the United States. Until its limitations became apparent in recent years, financial managers and analysts drew on it extensively for guidance in the inflationary environment that was so new to them. We outline the main propositions of the standard theory for comparison with recent developments in the economy and in economic theory. Inflation for our purposes means a rise in a general index of all prices causing depreciation in the purchasing power of a dollar.

THE DISTINCTION BETWEEN UNANTICIPATED AND ANTICIPATED INFLATION

Depreciation in the real value of money and other financial assets redistributes wealth and income and affects economic behavior. In analyzing the effect on behavior, the standard theory stresses a distinction between unanticipated and anticipated inflation. If inflation is unanticipated, dollar prices fixed by contract do not compensate for the subsequent decline in real value of the dollar. If inflation is anticipated, contract prices are set at the time of negotiation in such a way as to allow for the anticipated depreciation in real value or are adjusted during the period of the contract according to some index of inflation. A "complete" adjustment, if accurate, succeeds in keeping the real value unchanged during inflation, and financial decisions based on real values are not affected. These basic propositions of the standard theory, with due allowance for prevailing institutional practices, can account for many of the observed effects of inflation.

To explain these effects, the literature focuses on the question, Who gains and who loses from inflation, and what do they do about it?

When inflation is unanticipated, the answer to the first part of the question is fairly clear. Holders of money and other fixed-dollar financial instruments lose purchasing power. The gains accrue to the issuers of those assets—the government, which issues money and securities, and business firms, which issue bonds and other market instruments—while there will also be indirect gains to owners or beneficiaries of these firms. Financial intermediaries are not supposed to be much affected, since their assets and liabilities are both largely fixed in dollar terms.[3] Households gain insofar as they are borrowers, but the household sector as a whole is a net creditor to other sectors.

When inflation proceeds with all prices rising proportionately, *relative* prices are unchanged, and the allocation of income and resources is not altered. But proportional increases in prices are not the rule, of course, and different sectors of the economy gain or lose depending upon the pattern of relative price changes. It was once widely believed that wages lag behind output prices in inflation, redistributing national income from wages to profits[4] and thus providing a stimulus to business saving and investment. Wages do exhibit a slow response to accelerations and decelerations of inflation,[5] but studies that have reexamined this question do not find a systematic shift between labor and business income due to inflation.[6] Because no firm evidence exists of systematic lags in wages or any other group of prices, such lags have not played a part in the standard theory.

Although nonfinancial businesses are now thought *not* to gain from a wage lag, most of them are net debtors in their fixed-dollar contracts and in that respect gain from unanticipated inflation. Capital gains and wage lags aside, however, the standard theory supposes that inflation is largely neutral for the relation between output prices and costs. Such neutrality underlies the traditional view that business equity will remain intact during inflation and that common stocks will rise in dollar value more or less in proportion to the general price level. (The inadequacy of this presumption is discussed later.)

What are the effects of gains and losses from unanticipated inflation? Gains and losses within the private economy as a whole largely cancel each other, since they differ only by the net amount of claims on the government and foreigners. Some groups will lose, however, and they may want to make up the reduction in their real net worth by saving more. Nevertheless, an increase in saving by one sector is no guarantee that aggregate saving will increase. A redistribution of real income due to inflation will not affect the aggregate rate of consumption and saving in the economy unless the gainers and losers save at different rates from marginal changes in income. There is usually little basis for concluding that any such differences work one way or the other. It is sometimes thought that, if the initial gainers were businesses, they might retain part of the gains for internal expansion, in which case aggregate saving and investment in the economy would rise. That is one of the main reasons behind the once popular view, now widely doubted, that inflation fosters capital investment and economic growth. The trouble with such an argument is that other outcomes are equally conceivable. Unless the owners (stockholders) desire the implicit increase in the saving done for them by their businesses through increases in retained earnings and capital investment, they would reduce their saving in other forms to offset it.

In the initial stages of an inflation, those who recognize it can try to escape the consequences of a depreciation in the real value of money and other fixed-dollar assets. They can shift accumulated holdings and new acquisitions away from assets for which the real rates of return would be lowered by inflation. The shift would continue until real returns, pecuniary and nonpecuniary, of all holdings were equal on the margin. The standard theory envisages a transition period in which the adjustments are undertaken and then a final equilibrium position when the adjustments have been completed. The transition period could be rapid, or it could be drawn out if anticipations of inflation form slowly or if adjustments are delayed by institutional constraints such as long contracts and laws against usury.

Most of the attention devoted to these adjustments has focused on the demand for real money balances. In the theory, these adjustments to anticipated inflation reduce real money balances and thereby increase their marginal convenience yield until it equals the higher anticipated cost of holding money. The reduction in real balances is accomplished by a one-time increase in the price level resulting from an increase in aggregate expenditures and upward pressure on prices as the public offers unwanted balances in bidding for other goods and assets. A rise in prices to a new higher trend path can reduce real money balances by the desired amount. After the transition to the new trend path, prices continue rising at a rate that, given the growth rate of the money stock, keeps real money balances on their desired path. In all but severe inflations, however, the amount of the initial adjustment in real balances to a new trend path appears to be small.

The shift in demand away from money balances will initially be directed toward goods that are expected to maintain their real value during inflation and can also serve as partial substitutes for the store-of-value function of money. Such goods are real estate, physical capital including durable consumer goods, and basic commodities subject to minor physical depreciation. At first during the transition period, the demand for these goods will increase, and their relative prices will rise. The changes in relative prices elicit responses on the supply side. If supplies of these goods are elastic, production will expand, eventually pulling their relative prices back to their long-run relative costs of production.[7] The main exception is land, which is fixed in quantity (aside from the fact that it can be upgraded). The total value of the outstanding stocks of assets that substitute for money will remain higher in the final equilibrium through a combination of price and quantity increases, largely replacing the amount of real money balances eliminated from the public's holdings. The real quantity of money is largely determined by the public, given the nominal amount supplied by the monetary authorities. In the standard theory, common stocks play the same role as physical assets, reflecting a presumption that real business profits will not be affected by inflation. If the public shifts from money to common stocks, the theoretical consequences for long-run equilibrium are the same as for other assets. The price of stocks in real terms will rise. To the extent that corporations find the higher price of stocks attractive compared with other forms of financing and therefore issue more shares, the price will fall back, and the increased total real value outstanding will reflect mainly a larger "quantity" of stocks (number of shares), with the real value per share largely unchanged. There are numerous qualifications to this theoretical outcome, particularly due to taxes, but we ignore them here. The main point for present purposes is that desired shifts in asset holdings by the public produce corresponding, though not necessarily equal, shifts in supply.

Since the reduction in real money balances due to anticipated inflation is estimated to be slight for moderate rates of inflation, the resulting shift in demand to any given group of other assets will be quite small, perhaps undetectable in the data. The potential source of major shifts to other assets resides instead in the large amount of outstanding financial assets fixed in dollar terms. According to the standard theory, the effect of inflation on these holdings is different from that on money balances. Unlike money, on which the pecuniary rate of return is taken to be zero,[8] financial assets pay interest, and the interest rate can rise to compensate for the anticipated rate of inflation. An anticipated depreciation in the real value of outstanding fixed-dollar financial assets leads to an initial shift by buyers away from such assets. Consequently, their prices fall, and their nominal yields therefore rise. The result is a higher coupon rate than before on new issues. Any differences among various assets in real return to holders could be only a transitional phenomenon, except possibly for changes in risk or uncertainty, which are ignored in this analysis.

The effect of inflation on interest rates was studied at the turn of the century by Irving Fisher,[9] and his findings have come to be called the "Fisher effect." It is clearly a powerful force at work in inflationary economies. Nominal interest rates on new fixed-dollar instruments rise and compensate lenders for the anticipated depreciation in purchasing power of the principal and interest. If the return on real capital does not change, borrowers can offer a nominal interest rate higher by the amount of the anticipated rate of inflation. The rise in nominal interest rates continues until real rates of return on all fixed-priced assets are the same as those on variable-priced assets. In the standard theory, equilibrium nominal interest rates and the anticipated rate of inflation change by equal amounts (apart from the effect of taxes and institutional impediments).[10]

After the adjustment in nominal interest rates is completed, anticipated inflation affects neither real rates of return nor the relative demands for fixed-dollar financial assets (except for money balances) and other real assets. The dollar prices of previously issued securities declined, of course, when market interest rates rose in anticipation of inflation. This reduced the value at current market prices of outstanding bonds held in portfolios. But no one is induced after this adjustment to sell or avoid fixed-dollar assets because of more attractive real yields elsewhere. The decline in current market price was an adjustment for the anticipated erosion of the purchasing power of bonds at maturity. Old securities, at the reduced prices, thus carry an increased market yield to maturity equal to the higher nominal coupon rate on new securities; and the yields on both compensate for the anticipated rate of inflation.

What then underlies the popular notion that inflation encourages investors to shift from fixed-dollar assets to equity and other variable-priced assets and to borrow more? In the standard theory, such behavior only occurs during the transition period, when money balances are being reduced in real terms and nominal interest rates do not yet fully reflect the higher rate of inflation anticipated by some groups. (Hedging, discussed later, is not part of the standard theory.) If one group is liquidating assets at prevailing prices, some other group must be willing to acquire them; after all, someone is on the other side of every transaction. The selling group wants to avoid holding securities in anticipation of a decline in security prices—rise in nominal yields—which buyers do not foresee or which they expect to be smaller than that expected by sellers.

When everyone anticipates inflation at a new higher rate, securities have no buyers at the old price. Their prices decline, and nominal yields rise sufficiently to induce someone to hold each outstanding interest-bearing asset. There is no actual shift by the market as a whole from one kind of outstanding asset to another (which is impossible), but only an initial desired shift resulting in a change in market values. The relative prices of real estate and common stocks and physical capital might be bid higher transitionally. Permanently, they will rise only by the amount of the (minor) reduction in real money balances and, even then, only to the extent that supplies are not perfectly elastic. Although outstanding fixed-dollar securities have fallen in price, new securities bear a sufficiently higher yield to make them as attractive to savers as such securities were before inflation was anticipated.

What is true for individuals is also true for financial intermediaries which borrow on demand or short maturity to acquire a portfolio of long-term securities. These institutions might well face a rocky road during the transition period to a higher anticipated inflation rate. The rise in market interest rates imposes balance sheet losses on their portfolios, while their customers are attracted to market instruments paying higher yields than the institutions are able to meet at the time. When adjustments have been completed and portfolios turned over, however, the intermediaries can then pass on the higher coupon rates to customers, and their competitive position is the same as before.

In summary, anticipated inflation supposedly leaves the economy little affected in real terms aside from distortions due to taxes and ceilings. Nominal interest rates rise to compensate for the anticipated rate of inflation, and households have no reason to alter their holdings of financial and real assets. As a result, financial intermediaries maintain their position in the financial structure. The only exception is that inflation increases the cost of holding dollar assets on which no interest is paid—currency and, to some extent, demand balances. The real value of these assets will be reduced, but everything else, once adjustments are complete, is unchanged in real terms.

UNCERTAINTY AND HEDGING

The standard theory of the effects of inflation, with its narrow emphasis on the consequences of depreciation in the real value of fixed-dollar assets, is a generalized description of particular forces at work under inflationary conditions. It largely neglects institutional constraints, lags, and imperfect adjustments. It certainly does not incorporate all that was known about inflation even before the mid-1960s.

One major consideration that somehow never became an integral part of the standard theory is uncertainty, though writers were long aware of it. Inflation rarely proceeds at a steady rate for very long. Even in the recent moderate inflationary experience of the United States, the quarterly rate of inflation has often halved or doubled within a year's time. Such variations in the rate are extremely difficult to forecast. The experience of many countries indicates that as inflation becomes more severe, the magnitude of the variation increases.[11] As a result, the public does not focus on a single anticipated rate of inflation, but on a range of rates with varying chances of occurring. Uncertainty over what the rate will be creates a desire to hedge against undesirable outcomes. A nominal interest rate that is high enough to cover the anticipated rate of inflation still provides no protection for security buyers against an actual inflation rate that exceeds the anticipated one and provides no protection for issuers against a rate below the anticipated one.

The uncertainty created by an inflationary environment is not readily avoided, and no prescribed way exists for financial markets to respond to it. Modern theories of investment behavior are based on the existence of a riskless asset. In an inflationary environment, where no asset, including government money, is without risk to its real value, the general results of that theory no longer hold.[12] There is no longer a uniformly prescribed market assessment of the risk attached to each asset. Consequently, investors will differ in their perceptions of the risk of particular assets and of the risk premiums they will pay. Nonetheless, inflation was thought to impart a special attraction as hedges [13] to those assets, such as common stocks, that are expected to keep up with inflation and maintain the same value in real terms. The great uncertainty over future rates of inflation, together with an apparently uncritical faith in the protection afforded against inflation by equity, probably accounts for the initial attraction to the public of certain securities, such as convertible bonds, which increased in supply and popularity during the 1960s. Although corporations had special reasons to issue convertible debt in the 1960s,[14] these bonds were attractive chiefly as hedges against uncertainty. The yields on straight bonds, which reflected the market's anticipated rate of inflation, were higher than those on convertibles and would have been more attractive if the anticipated rate had been certain. The hedging attraction is also found in bonds linked to a price index, which are issued in some foreign countries and have been proposed for the United States.

The implications of uncertainty for economic behavior, which now receive considerable attention in the economic literature, extend the standard theory described above in an important direction. Given uncertainty over the rate of inflation, investors, hoping to protect themselves against unexpectedly high rates, may prefer equity and real assets to financial assets fixed in dollar terms *even when* nominal interest rates on financial assets compensate buyers for the rate of inflation anticipated as most likely. Issuers may prefer equity *even when* the anticipated inflation compensates for the high nominal interest rate they must pay on straight debt. The market value of equity and real assets outstanding would as a result be comparatively larger under inflationary conditions, subject to the qualification that increased risk could reduce the total demand to hold all assets. The extent of the increase in value of real assets would depend upon the degree of uncertainty over possible rates of inflation, rather than the point estimate of the anticipated rate. It is a rationale for the popular notion of a shift to equity during inflation. The "shift" would produce an increase in the market values in real terms of total holdings of equity securities and real assets and in the flow supply of new issues. This reason for a preference for equity seemed for a time to rest on firmer ground than the older common view that inflation stimulated economic activity and improved business profits in real terms.

To the uncertainty over future rates of inflation one must add the related uncertainty over future rates of interest. While nominal rates of interest are clearly affected by anticipations of inflation, changes in rates may not be completely synchronized with changes in anticipations and therefore may be an independent source of uncertainty. One reason for such changes in rates is government action against inflation, which has had some very violent short-run effects on interest rates, as in 1966, 1969, and 1974. The market faces the problem of anticipating not only the rate of inflation but also the type and extent of government reaction to inflation. An apparent example of such anticipation of government reaction is the seemingly perverse response of stock prices to news of rapid growth in the money supply, in which the market bypasses any direct effect of the increase in monetary growth and responds instead to an expectation of subsequent credit tightening to slow the increase.

It is not inconsistent with the standard theory to take account of inflation uncertainty by supposing that investors hedge against risks. Uncertainty means that the actual outcome of inflation will produce surprises, and unanticipated capital gains or losses will occur. In this view, inflation has effects in real terms by producing a preference for assets that mitigate the uncertainty of inflation. In theory, real assets and equity securities are inflation hedges and would be held and issued in larger volume relative to fixed-dollar assets. This would reduce the role of financial intermediaries which deal primarily in fixed-dollar instruments. The problem remains, however, that this extension of the standard theory does not account for the contrary developments since the mid-1960s.

NOTES

1. "Just as a toll can be levied on the use of roads or a turnover tax on business transactions, so also on the use of money. The higher the toll and the

tax, the less traffic on the roads and the less business transacted, so also the less money carried." Keynes [1923], ch. II, pt. I, "Inflation as a Method of Taxation," p. 49.

2. See the discussion in Kessel and Alchian [1962], Conard [1964], pt. II; and the first part of Lintner [1973].

3. Commercial banks receive special attention in the theory of inflation, because the tax on money balances due to anticipated inflation produces a revenue for the issuers of money—commercial banks and the government. See Cagan [1972], ch. 2.

4. In many of the business cycle theories reviewed by Haberler [1943], an initial lag of wages behind prices helps propel cyclical expansions; later, a catching-up rise in labor costs contributes to the onset of contraction. Also see the discussion of the literature in Kessel and Alchian [1960].

5. On the post–World War II period, see Wachter [1976], and Moore [1973].

6. See Kessel and Alchian [1960], Cargill [1969], and Lintner [1973].

7. According to modern growth theory, such changes in quantities of capital goods can have an effect, though presumably small for mild inflations, on the long-run real rate of return on capital.

8. To the extent that bank services on demand deposits are expanded and contracted similarly to changes in interest rates, demand deposits also pay a variable (nonpecuniary) return and are not a special case. For evidence on the effect of changing services on demand deposits, see Klein [1974].

9. The most complete statement of this work was published later in Fisher [1930].

10. Qualifications to the Fisher effect pertain first to taxes and second to statutory constraints. (1) Income taxes on interest income interfere with the adjustment. Lenders can be fully compensated for anticipated inflation after taxes only if the nominal interest rate, *after* deducting the applicable marginal tax rate, increases sufficiently to cover the inflation rate. Corporate borrowers can afford to pay an interest rate that compensates lenders after taxes for inflation, because such payments are deductible from the (generally higher) corporate income tax. See Gandolfi [1976], and Feldstein [1976]. (2) Some government regulations impose ceilings on nominal interest rates. State usury laws limit mortgage and installment loan rates, and federal regulations limit rates payable on time and savings deposits and prohibit interest on demand deposits.

It is not clear how serious the qualifications are in practice. Tax rates, though in many cases fairly high, are mitigated by less than universal coverage; municipal bonds are free of federal taxes and financial institutions pay low income tax rates. Interest ceilings are not unchangeable but are eventually raised. In general, however, the effects of taxes cannot be ignored.

11. See Okun [1971], and Logue and Willett [1976].

12. Lintner [1969], esp. section II.

13. In his classic book on investing, John Burr Williams viewed common stocks as an inflation hedge but was also aware of many qualifications. See Williams [1938], pp. 109-11.

14. Piper and Arnold [1977], pp. 280-82.

Chapter Two

What We Have Learned
Since the Mid-1960s

Central to all the departures from the standard theory is the fact that the market has *failed to develop* an asset that serves as a satisfactory hedge against inflation. Common stocks were once thought the prime asset to provide this hedge, but they have been inadequate over the past decade. This failure affects not only direct investments in corporate equity but also the kind of secondary instruments developed by financial intermediaries for indirect investment. Real property, aside from one family homes, has not been a practical substitute for most investors.

The notion, popular in the 1950s and 1960s, that corporate equity is a good hedge against changes in the general price level has been severely battered. Since the mid-1960s, equity prices have been subject to sharp declines in dollar value several times, and, though dollar prices have subsequently recovered each time, the real value of equities has fallen substantially. At the same time, the persistence and magnitude of inflation since the mid-1960s, though unusual for the United States, has led the public to believe that it is not a passing phenomenon. Expectations of inflation and of the continuing instability of the economy under inflation undoubtedly lie behind the decline in stock market values.

Several different types of equity-linked financial instruments reached a peak of importance in the late 1960s and then lost appeal. Convertible bond issues were greatest in value, at around $4 billion a year, and as a proportion of total corporate offerings, over 15 percent, in 1967-1969.[1] The proportion of new commercial mortgage commitments by large life insurance companies that included income or equity features rose in each year from 1965 to 1969-1970, reaching over 50 percent, but declined sharply to perhaps 10 percent by early 1973.[2] Private placements of debt issues that included equity kickers increased substantially in 1968 and 1969 and then receded, falling by 1972 to almost the pre-1968 proportion of the total volume.[3] Clearly the appeal and growth of these instruments reflected in part a concern over the uncertainty of the rate of inflation and a belief that equity values would keep up with whatever inflation rate might occur. The subsequent decline of their appeal after 1969 reflected, perhaps, a belief that the variability of inflation would diminish, but also, probably more important, a general disillusionment with equity as a hedge against inflation.

The uncertainty and the lack of a practical hedge against inflation have led investors to depart considerably from the behavior of the standard theory and from simple modifications of that theory that incorporate hedging. In the framework of the standard theory, an acceleration of inflation such as began in 1965 would be unanticipated at first, producing capital losses for creditors and capital gains for debtors; then anticipations would gradually catch up with developments and bring a corresponding increase in nominal interest rates. Nominal interest rates have in fact risen appreciably, perhaps sufficiently to compensate for the rate of inflation generally anticipated. (The success of the standard theory in predicting this development is important and should not be underrated.) Given a full adjustment of nominal interest rates to inflation, the standard theory predicts that no major shifts in saving patterns should occur. Given uncertainty over the inflation rate, however, shifts for hedging purposes from fixed-dollar to real assets should occur. Yet such shifts have been slight, and others have gone in the "wrong" direction toward fixed-dollar liquid assets. The uncertainty of inflation has not produced the consequences that the standard theory, as modified for hedging, implies should occur.

This theory is not wrong given the conditions it assumes to prevail. But it neglects important characteristics of inflationary movements and their consequences. The following sections review financial developments since the mid-1960s which are at least partly the consequences of inflation, although other factors may also have been at work. We take up the consequences for business firms first, because developments in the trend of earnings under inflation affect stock values. That has consequences for household saving and portfolios, which are crucial in turn to the fortunes of financial intermediaries. After government borrowing is briefly reviewed, a final section sums up the consequences for interest rates of the responses of the various sectors to the inflation-related developments.

FINANCIAL BEHAVIOR OF SECTORS

Business Firms

The popular belief that inflation benefits businesses is based on presumed lags in the transmission of inflation: An increase in aggregate demand is thought to raise prices of final goods and services and to increase the derived demand for inputs. If input prices and wages do not rise immediately, profit margins in the meantime expand. Costs are thought to rise to a position of equilibrium in relation to output prices gradually. Thereafter, to the extent that the course of inflation is anticipated, the effect on business profits is supposedly neutral as prices and costs rise proportionately in equilibrium.

The sequence for most manufacturing firms, however, appears to be just the opposite. As many studies have found, prices appear to be set to cover standard unit costs of production and are increased generally *after* costs rise.[4] An increase in demand first leads to an expansion of output, which is fed back to earlier stages of production as an increase in demand for input factors. Profits may at first rise, because the expansion of output absorbs available excess capacity and reduces costs of production per unit. As the expansion in output spreads through the economy, however, it elicits price increases in some products, particularly basic materials, and eventually raises wages. The price and wage increases travel forward through the production pipeline and raise costs. If materials prices rise rapidly, as in 1973, they may raise output prices faster than wages, which catch up later. The rising costs push up prices at each stage of production, but in the process, profit margins are on the average depressed.

When multiplying price increases make it evident that inflation is escalating, government policies are instituted to curb inflation. These initially curtail demand across the economy. Profit margins now deteriorate further and more drastically, because of the resulting decline in output, long before they benefit from a slowing of cost increases. Since 1965, monetary policy has contributed to a slowing of aggregate demand in 1967, 1970, and 1974–1975. In the second and third of these episodes, business recessions occurred, and one almost occurred in 1967. Although the slack markets removed the upward demand pressure on prices, inflation decelerated slowly because cost increases continued working through the economy, reflecting a delayed catch up to earlier pressures and anticipations of further inflation. Yet because of slack markets, price increases could not match the rise in standard unit costs, and profit margins, even for standard levels of output, were squeezed. In certain industries, profit margins were depressed further by government regulation of prices, which delayed the adjustment to cost increases. Regulation increased under the inflationary conditions of the early 1970s, as, for example, in the imposition of comprehensive controls in 1971 and the later tightening of controls on oil and gas prices. As a result of lower profit margins and reduced output, total real profits fell.

An escalation of inflationary pressures, therefore, brings in succession two contractionary influences to bear on profits. First, while under stable prices profits normally rise until near the end of a business expansion, a surge of inflation appears first in materials prices and other costs of resources and holds down the nominal increase in profits and reduces profits in real terms. Second, subsequent policies to subdue inflation contract business activity, further depressing profits. Only in the early stages of a business expansion, when inflation is relatively moderate and output is recovering, do profits rise strongly in real terms. One indication of these influences is the higher profit rate in 1965, during a non-inflationary cyclical expansion, than in 1968–1969 or 1972–1974, when rapid inflation accompanied the expansions (see Figure 2-1, series 1, page 26).

The foregoing discussion has been in terms of profits as conventionally measured. However, inflation alters the valuation of business assets and produces capital gains or losses, most of which conventional accounting disregards. To incorporate this effect of inflation, we must digress to adjust the profits data. Four adjustments may be made, three of which affect profits measured in current prices as well as in constant prices, and one of which is designed to express profits in dollars of constant purchasing power. Those that affect profits in current dollars are the corrections for (1) increases in the replacement cost of capital assets and inventories; (2) capital gains on tangible assets; and (3) changes in the market price of outstanding debt. The other is (4) the correction of dollar amounts to take account of general price inflation.

1. *Increases in the replacement cost of capital assets and inventories.* Historical cost accounting tends to misstate operating profits from an economic standpoint because allowances for the depreciation of capital and the cost of materials reflect acquisitions at earlier dollar prices which no longer prevail for new acquisitions. Last in-first out accounting (LIFO) largely corrects this understatement of the cost of materials used, but most corporations still use the misleading first in-first out method (FIFO). On this account, historical cost accounting in an inflation overstates profits and increases income taxes in real terms.

In the recent revisions of the national income data by the Department of Commerce, capital consumption was adjusted to put it on a current price basis, thus taking account of the effects of inflation and relative price changes on the value of the depreciable capital stock. In addition, this capital consumption adjustment removed the effects of accelerated depreciation on business accounts, as the earlier introduction of the inventory valuation adjustment removed the effect of price changes on the cost of materials.

2. *Capital gains on tangible assets.* If the replacement cost or price of capital goods rises or falls by more than the general price level, there is a need not only for adjusting depreciation, noted in (1), but also for entering a capital gain or loss. The firm has the use of a capital good or land that is worth more or less than was paid for it; the new price represents the current resource cost of using the capital. To recognize the change in price, the value of the capital good should be written up or down to produce a nonrecurring capital gain or loss which should be reflected in the profits and net worth of the firm, even if segregated as an extraordinary adjustment. Current practice is to record these changes in value only when the asset is sold. A full accounting for the effects of price changes requires the recognition of such changes in the period in which they occur, whether or not a purchase or sale takes place.[5]

3. *Changes in the market price of outstanding financial assets and liabilities.* The rise or decline of interest rates, as a result of inflation or other causes, will alter the current dollar value of a firm's outstanding financial assets and liabilities. For example, a rise in the anticipated rate of inflation, which causes interest rates to rise, reduces the dollar value of a firm's outstanding debt. Changes in the market value of outstanding securities, like those in prices of capital goods, affect the current net worth of a going firm and generate capital gains or losses to the firm.

It might be objected that the gain or loss to the firm of a change in market value of debt due to changes in interest rates cannot be realized unless the debt is retired and refunded at the new interest rate. For, if the debt is serviced until maturity, the ultimate dollar value at redemption is not affected by changes in market interest rates during its lifetime. That is a mistaken view, however. The capital gain is there, whether realized by refunding or not. A firm has gained by having issued its securities before a rise in interest rates occurs. Having contracted the loan at the previous low rate, the firm is worth more than a firm that is alike in other respects but has issued debt at the new higher rate. (This gain in the market value of borrowed funds is equivalent to that noted above for resources whose market value has increased.) Year by year, as the bond approaches maturity, the benefit to the firm of having borrowed earlier at a lower interest rate appears in profits as a lower interest cost than the firm would otherwise have to pay. If this benefit is recorded as a one-time capital gain in the dollar price of the bond at the time the price fell, subsequent yearly increases in the dollar price as it rises to its par redemption value are recorded as capital losses. These subsequent capital losses cancel the year-by-year contribution to profits of the lower-than-market interest cost paid by the corporation. After these adjustments, profits are increased initially by the capital gain when interest rates rise and are not affected thereafter; there occurs no double counting of the contribution to profits of lower interest rates.

Changes in market interest rates are reversible, of course, and the rates usually fluctuate more than do prices of capital goods. An adjustment for each movement could impart large fluctuations to net worth over time. In practice, such fluctuations could be avoided by assigning reversible changes in net worth to a special fund, from which transfers to regular net worth were made gradually over time.

4. *General price inflation.* Inflation reduces the real value of financial assets and liabilities and thus produces gains and losses that are traditionally disregarded in measuring profits. Most corporations, particularly nonfinancial corporations, have more financial liabilities than financial assets and thus, in inflation, gain in real terms from the depreciation in the purchasing power of their net financial liabilities. Recognition of this depreciation requires adding the decline in real value of financial liabilities to profits and deducting the decline in real value of financial assets, which, like the depreciation of tangible assets, is a cost to the firm.

It is sometimes objected that, unless a decline in the real value of debt is realized by a sale or redemption, it should not be added to current profits. The addition may be necessary, however, to correct an understatement that occurs even without a sale. Insofar as inflation comes to be anticipated, nominal interest rates rise to compensate lenders for the depreciation in real value of loans. While the higher interest paid by a firm on this borrowing is a deduction from its profits, the offsetting depreciation in the real value of this debt due to inflation is usually ignored. This is illogical. Part of business borrowing can be viewed as a replacement to the flow of internal funds for the payment of additional nominal interest, which compensates for the depreciation, due to inflation, of outstanding debt. The replacement leaves profits and net worth unchanged in real terms, though such debt depreciation does not show up in the conventional sources and uses of funds. (If nominal interest rates do not rise to compensate fully for the inflation rate, the firm has a net benefit, which adds to profits, from the decline in real value of its debt.)

The same is true for assets, producing the opposite effects on profits; higher interest rates on financial assets compensate for depreciation in real value due to inflation. In the case of two financial assets, however, inflation losses cannot be recouped by higher nominal interest because no interest is explicitly paid. These assets are cash and accounts receivable, to the extent that higher interest is not implicitly recouped through a change in terms. Inflation in effect makes the holding and use of these assets more expensive in real terms, as if a tax had been levied on them. Holdings of the items taxed by inflation can be pared, but only so far. The cost to the firm is a continuing requirement to add to the dollar amount of these financial assets to maintain them at the same real level; the cost is either paid out of profits or passed on to customers through higher prices. As Lintner [1975] points out, if the cost is not covered by higher real prices, it reduces gross internal funds available for other purposes and raises borrowing requirements.

All the foregoing are adjustments to the current value of profits. However, current dollar amounts, even after adjustment, give a misleading impression of changes over time because of declines in the purchasing power of a dollar. To facilitate comparisons between years, we should translate the current values described above into real, or constant price, values by deflating by a general price index. We use the consumer price index, although some other general price index, such as the GNP deflator, would do as well and perhaps apply even better to business firms.

We summarize these adjustments in Table 2-1 by the experience of a hypothetical corporation. This example is based on the following assumptions: (1) the nominal amounts of cash, other financial assets, gross capital assets, and debt remain constant; (2) the price of capital goods rises 20 percent, while the general inflation rate is 10 percent; (3) there is a rise in the level of interest rates which decreases the market value of financial assets and debt. In the balance sheet, the first two columns show beginning and end-of-period values under conventional accounting practices, column (3) incorporates adjustments to current values, and column (4) is the adjusted current-value balance sheet deflated to account for the assumed 10 percent general rate of inflation. In the income statement, the first column reflects conventional accounting practice, the second incorporates adjustments in current prices, and in the third all the figures are deflated to take account of the general price level increase.

Table 2-1. Examples of Inflation Adjustments.

A. Hypothetical Balance Sheet

| | Current Dollars | | | Constant Dollars (market value in beginning-of-period prices) |
| | Conventional Practice | | Market Value | |
	Beginning of period (1)	End of period (2)	End of period (3)	End of period[a] (4)
Assets				
Cash	100	100	100	90
Other financial	1,000	1,000	900[b]	810
Fixed capital, gross	10,000	10,000	12,000[c]	10,800
Accumulated depreciation[d]	−2,000	−3,000	−3,600[c]	−3,240
Net fixed capital	8,000	7,000	8,400	7,560
TOTAL	9,100	8,100	9,400	8,460
Liabilities				
Debt	2,000	2,000	1,800[b]	1,620
Net Worth	7,100	6,100	7,600	6,840

B. Hypothetical Income Statement
(beginning to end of period above)

| | Current Dollars | | At Beginning-of-Period Prices[a] |
	Conventional (1)	Adjusted (2)	(3)
Sales minus direct costs and taxes	2,000	2,000	1,900[e]
Depreciation[d]	−1,000	−1,200	−1,080
Net Profit	1,000	800	820
Gain from rise in price of net capital goods	—	1,400[c]	560[f]
Loss from decline in market value of financial assets	—	−100[b]	−90
Gain from decline in market value of debt	—	200[b]	180
Loss from decline in beginning-of-period real value of cash and other financial assets	—	—	−110
Gain from decline in beginning-of-period real value of debt			200
Net Profit, including capital gains and losses		2,300	1,560

[a]Assuming 10 percent increase in general price level during period.

[b]Reduction in value from rise in interest rates.

[c]Increase in value of gross fixed capital and depreciation from 20 percent rise in cost of capital goods (in Part B, $8,400–$7,000 = $1,400).

[d]Depreciation at 10 percent per year.

[e]Average prices during year assumed to reflect half the full-year change in the general price level.

[f]Value of net capital at end of period in current dollars deflated to beginning of period ($7,560) minus net capital at end of period valued in beginning-of-period prices ($7,000).

18

While the real value of sales is 5 percent lower than the nominal value, real depreciation is larger because of the higher value placed on capital assets (20 percent in nominal terms, 10 percent in real terms). Profits (excluding capital gains and losses) are therefore 18 percent lower in real terms. However, capital gains add substantially to real profits. The market value of net fixed capital is $1,400 higher in nominal terms and $560 in real terms. Although the beginning of period real values of cash and financial assets are reduced by 10 percent ($110) in real terms as a result of the general inflation, and an additional $100 in nominal terms and $90 in real terms because interest rates rose, the real value of financial liabilities is lower by $380, partly as a result of the general inflation and partly from the rise in interest rates. As a result of all of these adjustments, real profits are calculated at $1,560 at beginning-of-period prices, in contrast to $1,000 by a conventional accounting.

This example covers most of the main adjustments produced by inflation, though it does not show likely changes in flows—such as increases in dollar revenues and costs—and in interest expenses when net debt is incurred at higher interest rates. Moreover, the effect of inflation on flows of funds can be quite different from that on income, because many of the adjustments to income do not directly and concurrently reflect changes in flows but affect assets and liabilities in real terms and show up only in future flows of funds.

While the effects on profits of general inflation are widely acknowledged as needing recognition,[6] those due to changes in relative prices of capital goods and in the dollar price of debt outstanding are controversial. The SEC has recently required large corporations under its jurisdiction to report on current replacement cost. The adjustment for changes in dollar price of debt has been estimated in a recent article[7] but has yet to receive wide endorsement.

What is the effect of these various adjustments on corporate profits? Table 2-2 gives annual estimates in 1964 dollars for the past two decades. Corporate profits after taxes in column (1) are based on the standard accounting treatment of depreciation and inventory costs. Column (4) shows profits adjusted to a national accounts basis—that is, eliminating the effects of inventory valuation changes, a correction that reduces profits in almost every year, and calculating capital consumption on a consistent current cost basis. The latter correction tends to reduce profits by removing the understatement of capital consumption that results from calculating the value of capital at historical cost, but it tends to increase profits by removing the effects of the liberalization of depreciation rules.

The estimates of profits in column (10) add to column (4) the loss in real value of net financial assets from the rise in the general

Table 2-2. Nonfarm Nonfinancial Corporations' Profits Including and Excluding Adjustments for the Effects of Inflation, 1955–1977. (billions of 1964 dollars)

	After-tax Profits Conventional Basis	Inventory Valuation Adjustment	Capital Consumption Adjustment	After-tax Profits National Accounts Basis	Change in Real Value of Net Financial Liabilities Face Value	Change in Real Value of Net Financial Liabilities Market Value	Real Capital Gains (+) or Losses (−) on Land	Real Capital Gains (+) or Losses (−) on Reproducible Tangible Assets	Change in Dollar Price of Debt Outstanding at Beginning of Year	Profits (National Accounts Basis) Adjusted for — Change in Real Value of Net Financial Liabilities (4)−(5)	Change in Real Value of Net Financial Liabilities and Tangible Capital (4)−(5)+(7)+(8)	Change in Real Value of Net Financial Liabilities, Tangible Capital, and Market Value of Long-term Debt (4)−(6)+(7) +(8)−(9)
	(1)	(2)	(3)	(4)	(5)	(6)	(7)	(8)	(9)	(10)	(11)	(12)
1955	26.5	−2.0	−2.4	22.1	−0.2	−0.2	4.0	6.9	−1.7	22.3	33.2	34.9
1956	26.3	−3.1	−3.4	19.8	−1.7	−1.7	3.5	8.1	−10.7	21.5	33.1	43.8
1957	24.3	−1.7	−3.6	19.0	−2.1	−1.7	3.1	−0.8	−0.1	21.1	23.4	23.1
1958	20.0	−0.3	−3.7	16.0	−1.4	−1.1	3.9	−3.8	+0.3	17.4	17.5	16.9
1959	24.8	−0.5	−3.1	21.2	−1.1	−1.0	4.3	−5.7	−7.1	22.3	20.9	27.9
1960	22.4	0.3	−2.4	20.3	−1.2	−0.9	2.2	−1.6	+2.4	21.5	22.1	19.4
1961	21.8	0.1	−1.9	20.0	−0.6	−0.5	4.5	−10.6	+1.2	20.6	14.5	13.2
1962	25.2	0.1	1.1	26.4	−1.2	−1.0	3.8	−5.1	+2.0	27.6	26.3	24.1
1963	27.5	−0.2	1.9	29.2	−1.7	−1.5	3.9	−2.8	−0.4	30.9	32.0	32.2
1964	32.5	−0.5	2.6	34.6	−1.1	−1.0	4.6	−0.6	+2.2	35.7	39.7	37.4
1965	38.3	−1.9	3.5	39.9	−2.3	−2.1	4.1	2.7	−2.5	42.2	49.0	51.3
1966	39.6	−2.0	3.6	41.2	−4.5	−4.0	3.0	5.6	−13.6	45.7	54.3	67.4
1967	36.5	−1.6	3.3	38.2	−4.7	−3.8	2.8	8.7	−6.8	42.9	54.4	60.3
1968	35.8	−3.0	3.3	36.1	−7.7	−6.1	0.9	11.8	−1.6	43.8	56.5	56.5
1969	31.2	−4.7	3.0	29.5	−10.7	−8.5	2.9	15.2	−22.8	40.2	58.3	78.9
1970	23.6	−4.1	1.3	20.8	−10.3	−7.1	1.9	11.8	+16.2	31.1	44.8	25.4
1971	27.0	−3.8	0.4	23.6	−6.8	−5.3	4.7	8.9	+19.1	30.4	44.0	23.4
1972	32.7	−4.9	2.0	29.8	−7.2	−6.4	8.1	11.0	+2.2	37.0	56.1	53.1
1973	39.6	−13.0	1.3	27.9	−19.3	−17.4	9.9	31.8	−16.0	47.2	88.9	103.0
1974	40.9	−25.4	−1.9	13.6	−28.2	−23.9	2.9	41.5	−25.0	41.8	86.2	106.9
1975	37.3	−6.9	−6.9	23.5	−17.9	−13.6	3.7	15.0	+20.6	41.4	60.1	35.2
1976	44.2	−7.7	−7.9	28.6	−11.7	−9.7	1.3	−1.0	+34.3	40.3	40.6	4.3
1977	46.3	−7.4	−8.7	30.2	−20.5	−19.8	1.4	29.9	−11.0	50.7	82.0	92.3

Notes:
  Col. (1) through (3): Profits Before Tax less Profits Tax Accruals plus Foreign Branch Profits, Inventory Valuation Adjustment and Capital Consumption

Table 2-2. (continued)

Col. (4): Sum of columns (1) through (3).

Col. (5): Nonfarm Nonfinancial Corporations' Financial Assets less Total Liabilities, end of preceding year, multiplied by the change in the monthly CPI from the end of the preceding year to the end of the current year to get the current value of changes in real net financial assets and then deflated by the annual average CPI. Data for 1955-1974 are from Flow of Funds Accounts, 1946-1975(December 1976); for 1975-1977 from unpublished FOF tables on Financial Assets and Liabilities: Nonfinancial Corporate Business Sector.

Col. (6): Same procedure as for column (5) except that the market value of long-term debt is substituted for the face value. The market value is estimated as the face value multiplied by the ratio of market to face value of long-term corporate bonds listed on the New York Stock Exchange. The market value calculation follows the method in Shoven and Bulow [1976]. Aggregate market and face values of bonds are from The New York Stock Exchange Fact Book.

Col. (7): 1955-1975: Total current dollar land values for the nation as a whole, deflated by year and values of the CPI, are used to derive a "real" price index for land on the assumption that the national land total is fixed and that all value changes represent price changes. The real price index is then applied to values, in 1964 dollars, of land held by nonfinancial corporations, to estimate capital gains on land in 1964 dollars. All land data are from Raymond Goldsmith's worksheets for the National Bureau project on the Measurement of Economic and Social Performance (MESP).

Since Goldsmith's estimates did not extend beyond 1975, the 1976 and 1977 figures are rough extrapolations. For the "real" change in the price of land, 1976, we used unpublished land value estimates by Helen Tice, now of the Bureau of Economic Analysis. The 1977 increase is estimated at 14.3 percent, assuming the same rate of growth as in the average of several previous years. Nonfarm nonfinancial corporate land was estimated for 1976 by assuming the same relation to Tice's corresponding figure (69.8 percent) as in earlier years and for 1977 by assuming a constant ratio to the value of structures.

Helen Tice's estimates of the value of nonfarm nonfinancial corporate land are higher than Goldsmith's and imply larger capital gains, as follows:

Annual Average Real Capital Gains on Land

	Table 2 (Goldsmith)	Tice	Difference
1955-64	3.8	5.8	2.0
1965-74	4.1	6.5	2.4
1975-76	2.5	6.8	4.3
Total	3.8	6.2	2.4

Col. (8): Differences between current and historical cost values of structures and equipment and of inventories held by nonfarm nonfinancial corporations, deflated by end-of-year levels of the CPI. Structures and equipment data are from Fixed Nonresidential Business and Residential Capital in the United States, 1925-75 (U.S. Department of Commerce, Bureau of Economic Analysis, June 1976), with some revisions and 1975-1977 data directly from the BEA. Inventory data are also directly from BEA.

Col. (9): The change in the difference between face value and market value of long-term debt of nonfarm nonfinancial corporations [see columns (5) and (6)] both deflated by the end-of-year CPI. Data are from Flow of Funds Accounts, 1946-1975 (December 1976), for 1955-1974; revised 1975 to 1977 data are directly from the Federal Reserve Board, Tables on Financial Assets and Liabilities: Nonfinancial Corporate Business Sector.

We have assumed that the market value of all long-term debt is affected by interest rate changes. If it were assumed that only bonds and mortgages, but not bank debt, were so affected, the amounts would be smaller. The following are the differences for a few of the years:

	Table 2	Assuming Constant Market Value of Bank Debt
1972	+2.2	+2.0
1973	-16.0	-13.3
1974	-25.0	-20.6
1975	+20.6	+16.3
1976	+34.3	+29.7

Col. (10): Profits adjusted to include real capital losses on financial assets and the real capital gains on liabilities from increases in the general price level.

Col. (11): Profits adjusted further to include real capital gains or losses on tangible assets.

Col. (12): Profits adjusted further to include real capital gains or losses on long-term debt from the changes in interest rates and also calculating gains on long-term debt from general price level increases on the basis of the market value rather than the face value of long-term debt.

price level, which added to profits in all years because the debts of nonfinancial corporations exceeded their financial assets. Column (11) adds in addition all real capital gains and losses resulting from price changes. These include the revaluation of land and reproducible tangible assets (to the extent that their price changes differed from those of the CPI), which added to profits in most years.

The controversial adjustment for changes in the market value of outstanding debt (item 3, above, and sixth line in Table 2-1, Part B) is made in column (12). This is the most volatile element of profit adjustment, swinging from large positive to large negative values with changes in interest rates.

Table 2-3 shows the net worth of nonfinancial corporations under different valuation methods. The first (A) is essentially the standard accounting valuation with financial assets and liabilities at face value and tangible assets at historical cost. The second (B) includes current valuations for tangible assets, but face values for others; and the third (C) is as close as we can come to a completely market valuation basis. Long-term debt is at market value, and tangible assets are at current cost. The short-term financial assets can be thought of as being at market value, assumed to be identical to face value.

The different concepts of profits and net worth give rise to several measures of the rate of return on net worth, shown in columns 4 through 8. The first is essentially a conventional accounting measure. The second uses the adjustments incorporated in the National Income and Product Accounts (NIPA) in the numerator (excluding inventory revaluations from profits and applying consistent depreciation rates on current values of plant and equipment) and correspondingly measures inventories and plant and equipment at current cost in the denominator. The third takes account of the erosion through inflation of the real value of financial assets and liabilities denominated in dollar terms. The fourth adds to the numerator capital gains and losses on tangible capital from changes in the real prices of inventories and of land, plant, and equipment. The fifth adds the effect of interest rate changes on the market value of long-term debt to the numerator and correspondingly values long-term debt at market in the denominator. Columns (9) through (11) show the market value of equity per unit of net worth, under the three alternative definitions of the latter. A brief survey of similar series recently presented in the literature is given in the Appendix.

Although column (8), incorporating all the adjustments, is more appropriate for assessing the total return to stockholders in any single year, each of the other columns is useful for distinguishing the effects of particular adjustments, the implications of particular accounting views, or the level of profitability one might project under different assumptions about inflation rates. For example, the wide fluctuations of column (8) presumably reflect the effects on interest rates of rises and declines in the rate of inflation. To project the latest profit rate under this concept would imply an expectation of a continuing rise or decline in the inflation rate, an unlikely assumption. A projection of the profit rate of column (5) is in a sense a conservative one, since it incorporates the effects of past inflation but not future inflation. A projection of column (6) incorporates a constant rate of general price level changes, but not any future real changes in specific land or plant and equipment prices, while a projection of column (7) would assume a continuation of past relationships between these prices and the general price level.[8]

Our insistence on the theoretical relevance of capital gains and losses to the measure of profits should not be construed as an endorsement of proposals that individual corporations be required to include all such adjustments in their reports of profits to the public. Complete current cost accounting would require estimates of the market values of individual capital goods, virtually impossible for an individual company to measure in view of changes in technology. It may be more practical for individual corporations to adjust historical costs for changes in some prescribed general index of prices, index of capital goods prices, or industry-specific capital goods price index, and to ignore any deviations of the prices of individual capital goods from the general indexes. This has the advantage of simplicity, yet allows for the major effects of inflation. The adjustment of aggregate data as in Table 2-2 does not escape the problems of current cost accounting, but it can be done adequately, even if crudely, for present purposes by ignoring the need for definiteness expected in company accounts. As noted earlier, however, recent SEC requirements point in the direction of requiring current cost accounting.[9]

Turning now to our estimated adjustments, we show, in Table 2-3 and Figure 2-1, the rate of return on corporate equity as conventionally reported and with the various adjustments for inflation. The adjustments have sizable effects on the levels of the rates of return, as is to be expected. The conventional rate in column (4) of Table 2-3 is substantially reduced when we shift to the NIPA concept of capital cost in column (5). The NIPA adjustment makes the rate lower throughout because it makes profits lower, except in 1962–1968 (Table 2-2), and net worth substantially higher. The decline in rates of return due to higher replacement costs is roughly offset, since the mid-1960s, by increases in rates of return due to declines

Table 2-3. Nonfarm Nonfinancial Corporations' Net Worth, Return on Net Worth, and Ratio of Market Value of Equity to Net Worth, 1954–1977

	Net Worth End of Year (billions of 1964 dollars)			Rate of Return — After-tax Profits (Table 2-2) as Percent of Net Worth (Table 2-3) at End of Preceding Year					Market Value of Equity per Dollar of Net Worth End of Year		
	A	B	C	Col. 1* A	Col. 4* B	Col. 10* B	Col. 11* B	Col. 12* C	Market Value A	Market Value B	Market Value C
	(1)	(2)	(3)	(4)	(5)	(6)	(7)	(8)	(9)	(10)	(11)
1954	227.5	304.8	305.2						1.138	0.850	0.848
1955	244.0	333.7	335.9	11.6	7.2	7.3	10.9	11.4	1.297	0.949	0.943
1956	255.4	356.7	369.5	10.8	5.9	6.4	9.9	13.0	1.288	0.922	0.890
1957	263.8	368.3	381.2	9.5	5.3	5.9	6.6	6.3	1.077	0.772	0.745
1958	271.5	374.8	387.4	7.6	4.3	4.7	4.8	4.4	1.411	1.022	0.989
1959	284.3	386.2	405.9	9.1	5.7	6.0	5.6	7.2	1.434	1.055	1.004
1960	284.5	385.6	403.0	7.9	5.3	5.6	5.7	4.8	1.391	1.026	0.982
1961	301.8	395.7	411.8	7.7	5.2	5.3	3.8	3.3	1.622	1.237	1.188
1962	314.7	406.3	420.4	8.3	6.7	7.0	6.6	5.9	1.360	1.054	1.018
1963	325.0	416.9	431.5	8.7	7.2	7.6	7.9	7.7	1.517	1.182	1.142
1964	340.2	434.9	447.2	10.0	8.3	8.6	9.5	8.6	1.574	1.232	1.198
1965	355.9	454.8	469.6	11.3	9.2	9.7	11.3	11.5	1.656	1.296	1.255
1966	366.3	473.1	501.5	11.1	9.1	10.0	11.9	14.4	1.435	1.111	1.048
1967	381.4	498.4	533.6	10.0	8.1	9.1	11.5	12.0	1.683	1.288	1.203
1968	383.1	512.2	549.0	9.4	7.2	8.8	11.3	10.6	1.883	1.408	1.314
1969	386.4	533.9	593.5	8.1	5.8	7.8	11.4	14.4	1.592	1.152	1.036
1970	380.6	545.0	588.4	6.1	3.9	5.8	8.4	4.3	1.530	1.069	0.990
1971	386.9	565.5	589.8	7.1	4.3	5.6	8.1	4.0	1.682	1.151	1.103
1972	397.9	593.1	615.2	8.5	5.3	6.5	9.9	9.0	1.786	1.198	1.155
1973	393.6	630.6	668.8	10.0	4.7	8.0	15.0	16.7	1.300	0.811	0.765
1974	383.3	669.4	732.5	10.4	2.2	6.6	13.7	16.0	0.810	0.464	0.424
1975	387.2	690.2	732.7	9.7	3.5	6.2	9.0	4.8	0.988	0.554	0.522
1976	408.5	710.5	718.7	11.4	4.1	5.8	5.9	0.6	1.098	0.632	0.624
1977	413.5	745.1	764.3	11.3	4.2	7.1	11.5	12.8	0.920	0.511	0.498

Table 2-3 (continued)

A   Conventional accounting method: financial assets and liabilities at face value, tangible assets at historical cost.

B   Financial assets and liabilities at face value, tangible assets at current cost.

C   Financial assets and short-term liabilities at face value, long-term liabilities at market value, tangible assets at current cost.

*Column numbers refer to Table 2-2.

Notes:

Col. (1): Financial assets and liabilities at face value from *Flow of Funds Accounts, 1946-1975* (December 1976), for 1954-1974; 1975-1977 data directly from the Federal Reserve Board, Tables on Financial Assets and Liabilities: Nonfinancial Corporate Business Sector. Reproducible tangible assets at historical cost from BEA [see notes to Table 2-2, column (8)]. Land at book value from *Statistics of Income*, Internal Revenue Service, with rough extrapolations assuming a constant rate of increase of $3 billion per year after 1972, the same rate as in the preceding five years. All series are deflated by the end-of-year CPI.

Col. (2): Financial assets and liabilities at face value from Flow of Funds data. Reproducible tangible assets at current cost from *Fixed Nonresidential Business and Residential Capital in the United States, 1925-75* (U.S. Department of Commerce, Bureau of Economic Analysis, June 1976), with some revisions and 1975-77 data directly from the BEA. Land at current value from Raymond Goldsmith's worksheets for the National Bureau project on The Measurement of Economic and Social Performance. All series are deflated by the end-of-year CPI.

Col. (3): Financial assets and short-term liabilities at face value from Flow of Funds data. It is assumed that there is little investment in long-term financial assets. Market value of long-term debt is estimated from the ratio of market to face value of bonds of U.S. companies traded on the New York Stock Exchange, from various issues of *The New York Stock Exchange Fact Book*, and from Shoven and Bulow [1976]. All series are deflated by the end-of-year CPI.

Cols. (4) through (8): Rates of return on net worth, based on various measures of after-tax profits in Table 2-2 and of net worth at end of preceding year in columns (1) through (3) of Table 2-3.

Cols. (9) through (11): Market value of all corporate equity is from Flow of Funds data. The market value of financial corporations' equity is assumed to be in proportion to the net worth of financial corporations relative to all corporations. The net worth of financial corporations is estimated from Flow of Funds data for financial assets and liabilities and BEA data for reproducible tangible assets. The corporate finance sector is assumed to consist of the following Flow of Funds subsectors: commercial banking, life insurance, other insurance, savings and loan associations, real estate investment trusts, brokers and dealers, open-end investment companies, and money market funds, ignoring the fact that some of these are not stock corporations. Denominator is net worth as used in columns (1) to (3) at current dollar value before deflation.

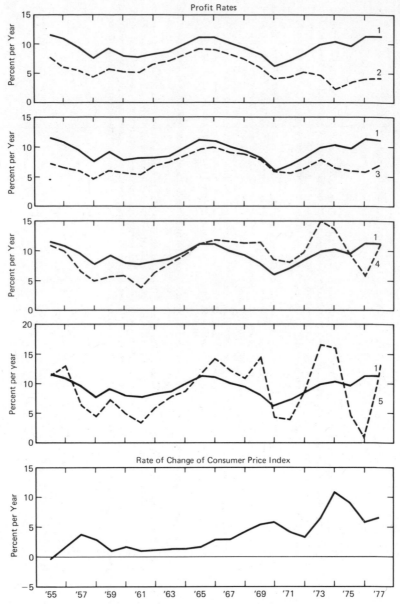

Source: Table 2-3 and Bureau of Labor Statistics, consumer price index, all items (year to year).

Note: Identification of profit rates in Table 2-3.
     1: Conventional accounting method (col. 4).
     2: Rate with Tangible assets adjusted for replacement cost (col. 5).
     3: Rate 2 *plus* change in real value of net financial liabilities (col. 6).
     4: Rate 3 *plus* capital gains or losses on tangible capital (col. 7).
     5: Rate 4 *plus* capital gains or losses in market value of long-term debt (col. 8).

Figure 2-1   Ratio of After-Tax Profits to Net Worth, with Various Adjustments for Inflation, and the Inflation Rate, 1955-1977

in the real value of net financial liabilities [column (6)]. These give a rate in 1975-1977 that is close to or above its level in 1959-1960 preceding the steep rise of the early 1960s. The adjustments for both tangible capital and financial gains and losses added in column (8) then raise the profit rate on the average, particularly in the period since the mid-1960s when real capital values and interest rates rose. These adjustments, particularly the latter, exhibit great variability in direction as well as magnitude from year to year and produce wide swings in rates of return. The corresponding rates for individual companies would, of course, show considerable diversity.

The rate of return, however measured, is highly dependent upon cycles in business activity. It is high in the vicinity of cyclical peaks and low near cyclical troughs. Its movements also give evidence of an adverse effect of inflation on operating profits. The rate of return was generally low in the late 1950s, after a decade of mild but persistent inflation. It then rose steadily during the price stability of the first half of the 1960s and fell in the inflationary second half of that decade. All the measures display the usual cyclical recovery following the 1970 recession. The 1973-1975 recession produced differences, however. The sharp rise in inflation in 1973-1974 improved the profit rate by conventional accounting but reduced it by the NIPA concept. It improved it moderately by the adjustments in column (6) and greatly by those in columns (7) and (8). While the size of the inflation adjustments then moderated, interest rate changes reduced the fully adjusted rate in column (8) dramatically in 1975-1976. As compared with 1972, the conventionally measured rate was quite high in 1976-1977, the NIPA rate was quite low, and the column (6) rate, incorporating the effects of general price level changes, was about the same. The fully adjusted rate on average was low in 1975-1976, but jumped above the 1972 level in 1977; the column (7) rate, which does not include the interest rate adjustments, was also higher in 1977 than in 1972.[10]

In general, therefore, the inflationary environment since the mid-1960s has reduced the real profit rate, however measured, from the high level reached during the price stability of the early 1960s. Since the end of the decline in 1970, the adjusted rates have on the average recovered moderately. At the same time, they have fluctuated considerably. Changes in the rate of inflation greatly affect all the measures of the profit rate, but not always in the same direction nor by the same amount. This adds to the uncertainty over the effect of inflation on profit rates.

The ratio of stock prices to net worth declined to a low level after 1972 (Figure 2-2), contributing significantly to the poor

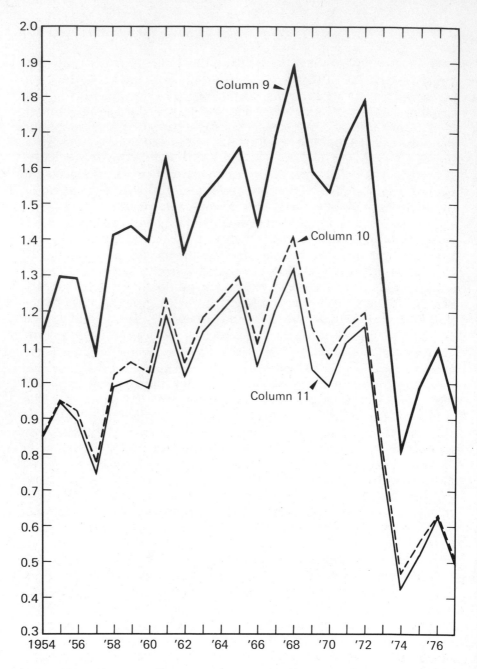

Source: Table 2-3.
Column 9:   Conventional accounting method.
Column 10:   Tangible assets at current cost.
Column 11:   Tangible assets at current cost and long-term debt at market value.

Figure 2-2.   Market Value of Equity per Dollar of Net Worth, 1954–1977

performance of stocks as a hedge against inflation. This decline reflected a broad reassessment by the market of the value of net worth. An associated decline also occurred in the price-earnings ratio—the market's valuation of current after-tax earnings.[11] For example, based on profits corrected for general price level changes (column 6) and net worth with debt at face value (column 10), the price-earnings ratio declined from 16 in 1955–1964 and 18 in 1972 to 7.5 in 1975 and recovered only to 9–10 in 1976–1977. Some decline in stock prices was likely after the mid-1960s because of the fall in profit rates; all measures of the profit rate declined from the mid-1960s to 1970. After 1970, the profit rate recovered to an extent that varies with the particular adjustments made for the effects of inflation. It is not clear to what extent market participants allowed for the various effects of inflation on corporate profits. If stock prices are interpreted as a reflection of earnings, the market seems to come closest to accepting the rate of return of column (6), including only general price level adjustments, in the sense that the price-earnings ratio on this basis fluctuates the least. Nevertheless, it does show a large reduction between 1955–1964 and 1975–1977. If stock prices are interpreted as a reflection of net worth, all the concepts show about the same range of valuations and all show low levels for recent years.

The sharp further decline in stock prices after 1972 suggests that the market saw these effects as generally reducing real profits. In any event, the decline in the price-earnings ratio after 1972 can be attributed to widely held expectations not only that profit rates were lower and would not rise much, but also that they would be subject to large fluctuations and were vulnerable to sharp setbacks whenever the rate of inflation stepped up. A low price-earnings ratio may well persist, therefore, because of the extreme uncertainty of profits in an inflationary environment.

These developments in profits and equity values had a largely predictable influence on corporate finances, as can be seen in Table 2–4, which shows the sources and uses of funds in real terms. Since 1964 marks the end of a period of relative price stability, averages are given for the decades 1955–1964 and 1965–1974; and for the recent years, 1975–1977. Gross internal funds of corporations (undistributed after-tax profits, less inventory gains, plus capital consumption in current prices) were high in 1965 compared with the preceding decade, but they did not grow substantially in the next decade, although they did then increase in 1975–1977. However, the replacement cost of capital and acquisitions of financial assets both grew rapidly. The financial squeeze was resolved by a

Table 2-4. Sources and Uses of Funds, Nonfarm Nonfinancial Corporations, 1965–1977. (billions of 1964 dollars)

PART A

| Year | Gross Internal Funds (1) | External Funds | | | | | Fixed Investment | | Change in Inventories (9) | Net Acquisition of Financial Assets (10) | Discrepancy (11) |
		Equity (2)	Bonds and Mortgages (3)	Other Debt (4)	Miscellaneous[a] (5)	Total[b] Funds (6)	Replacement (7)	Net (8)			
1965	55.3	-0.0	9.1	11.0	14.1	89.5	32.1	21.7	7.2	19.9	8.6
1966	57.8	1.2	14.1	9.1	10.4	92.7	33.9	26.1	12.6	12.1	8.0
1967	57.0	2.2	17.3	7.3	2.9	86.7	36.3	23.0	8.2	15.7	3.6
1968	55.6	-0.1	17.0	11.6	18.1	102.2	38.1	23.8	6.1	25.7	7.2
1969	52.2	2.9	14.7	15.0	15.7	100.5	40.2	24.8	7.1	24.0	4.4
1970	47.1	4.6	21.5	7.1	3.8	84.0	42.2	19.3	2.7	12.4	7.2
1971	52.6	8.8	23.2	3.6	10.8	98.9	44.4	18.4	2.8	22.1	10.7
1972	60.0	8.1	22.7	12.9	10.7	114.3	46.2	22.5	5.6	27.1	12.2
1973	58.6	5.5	20.6	24.8	17.4	126.9	47.6	27.8	9.3	28.7	11.3
1974	48.9	2.6	22.4	27.4	14.0	115.2	50.4	22.7	7.6	22.2	8.2
1975	62.2	5.7	22.7	-7.3	2.4	85.7	55.6	7.5	-7.0	19.4	9.3
1976	68.6	5.7	20.8	5.3	16.0	116.4	57.8	9.1	7.5	31.0	8.9
1977	69.9	4.5	22.2	17.3	18.4	116.2	59.1	3.7	7.8	40.7	4.9
Averages											
1955–1964	38.0	1.6	7.7	3.7	5.6	56.7	27.4	10.1	3.4	11.1	4.8
1965–1974	54.5	3.6	18.3	13.0	11.8	101.1	41.4	23.0	6.9	21.0	8.1
1975–1977	66.9	5.3	21.9	5.1	12.3	106.1	57.5	6.8	2.8	30.4	7.7

[a]Made up of Profit Taxes Payable, Trade Debt, and Miscellaneous Liabilities.

[b]Uses of Funds do not include Mineral Rights from U.S. Government; therefore, the sum of the uses may be less than Total Funds.

Table 2-4 (continued)

PART B

| | Annual Additions to Equity | | | | Additions to Debt Relative to Additions to Equity | | |
	Gross Internal Funds Minus Replacement Plus Equity	Revaluation of Land and Capital Assets	Book Value of Debt and Miscellaneous	Decline in Real Value of Net Financial Liabilities	$\frac{(3)}{(1)}$	$\frac{(3)}{(1)+(2)}$	$\frac{(3)+(4)}{(1)+(2)}$
	(1)	(2)	(3)	(4)	(5)	(6)	(7)
1955–1964	12.2	2.0	17.0	-1.2	1.4	1.2	1.1
1965–1974	17.0	19.0	43.1	-10.2	2.5	1.2	0.91
1975–1977	14.7	16.8	39.3	-16.7	2.7	1.2	0.72

Source: Table 2-2 and *Flow of Funds Accounts, 1946–1975* (December 1976), for 1965–1974; *Flow of Funds Accounts, 4th Quarter 1977* (February 1978), for 1975–1977, Tables on Saving and Investment: Nonfinancial Corporate Business Sector. Columns (7) and (9), Part A, and column (2), Part B, incorporate Department of Commerce adjustments of capital consumption and inventory valuation.

The columns in Part B are derived as follows:

(1) = col. (1) + col. (2) – col. (7)   (Part A)
(2) = col. (7) + col. (8)   (Table 2–2)
(3) = col. (3) + col. (4) + col. (5)   (Part A)
(4) = col. (5)   (Table 2–2)

lack of growth in net investment and increasing reliance on external funds. Equity financing expanded, but, given the decline in real share prices after 1968, this avenue was limited. Most of the increase in funds in the 1965–1974 decade, compared with the preceding one, was borrowed. This made corporations even more subject to the turbulence of an inflationary economy. During each round of monetary restraint to subdue inflation, financial markets tightened and became unreceptive to new bond issues, forcing many companies (and municipalities) at such times into an illiquid reliance on short-term debt requiring regular rollovers, followed by a period of massive refinancing into long-term debt as soon as conditions permitted. The cumulative disruption of these developments to normal business financing contributed, along with lower real profit rates and general uncertainty, to the impairment of corporate liquidity. The trend of declining liquidity ratios was reversed and some improvement accomplished only in the last few years.[12]

As a result of heavy borrowing, the debt-equity ratio as conventionally measured rose. This is demonstrated by the calculations of Part B of Table 2-4. By the conventional measure of column (5), additions to debt exceeded those to equity by 40 percent in the earlier decade but by well over 100 percent since then. If we include in equity additions from revaluations of capital assets, the difference between 1955–1964 and the succeeding decade is eliminated (column 6). If we also take account of the effect on debt of the decline in real value of net financial liabilities, the trend is reversed; the ratio of debt to equity financing declines. It turns out that much of the corporate borrowing was a replacement of depreciated debt and did not add to the debt-equity ratio.

To the extent that the decline in stock prices in recent years reflected a correction of the overvaluation of the mid-1960s, stocks might be expected to keep up with inflation in the long run. After the previous major inflation—World War II—stocks generally recovered their initial real value, but only over the long run. A study of twenty-four countries[13] for the period from the beginning of World War II to the end of the 1960s shows that while stocks did not maintain their purchasing power during the World War II inflation, they regained their prewar level of purchasing power eventually in a majority of the countries. Table 2-5, reproduced from the study, shows that rates of change in stock prices in real terms for the full period were positive for fourteen of the twenty-four countries. Stock prices kept up with inflation wherever the average inflation rate was no more than 4 percent. Where they did not keep up was mainly in the countries with the highest inflation rates—an average

Table 2-5.   Stock Values, Pre-World War II to 1969.

		Rate of Change[a] (percent per year)			
Country	*Period*	*Stock Values*	*Consumer Prices*	*Deflated Stock Values*	*Total Change in Deflated Stock Values (percent)*
Australia	1939–69	5.0	4.4	0.6	20
Austria	1937–69	9.5	7.4	2.0	92
Belgium	1939–69	4.8	5.8	−1.0	−25
Canada	1939–69	6.2	3.2	3.0	144
Denmark	1939–69	3.6	4.6	−1.0	−26
Finland	1939–69	9.9	10.5	−0.6	−16
France	1939–69	13.5	12.9	0.7	22
India	1939–69	1.4	6.2	−4.7	−76
Ireland	1939–69	5.4	4.5	0.9	29
Italy	1939–69	14.2	14.9	−0.7	−20
Japan	1936–69	10.5	18.9	−8.4	−94
Mexico	1939–69	7.1	7.5	−0.4	−12
Netherlands	1939–69	6.8	4.9	1.9	79
New Zealand	1939–69	4.9	3.7	1.3	46
Norway	1939–69	2.6	4.3	−1.6	−38
Peru	1939–69	0.8	10.3	−9.5	−94
Portugal	1939–69	4.4	4.1	0.4	12
South Africa	1939–69	6.8	3.5	3.4	175
Spain	1940–69	4.3	7.4	−3.1	−59
Sweden	1939–69	6.2	4.0	2.2	94
Switzerland	1939–69	4.4	3.0	1.5	55
United Kingdom	1939–69	5.9	4.3	1.6	61
United States	**1939–69**	**7.1**	**3.2**	**3.9**	**224**
Venezuela	1939–69	4.5	3.4	1.1	41

Source: International Monetary Fund, *Financial Statistics,* with some earlier data from United Nations, *Statistical Yearbook* and individual country reports. Reproduced from Cagan [1974a].

[a]Continuous compounding.

of 9 percent, as compared to 6.5 percent for all countries. Recovery to the prewar value of stocks occurred for the median country by the mid-1950s (not shown), a decade and a half after the beginning of the World War II inflation. If we apply the same period of recovery to recent experience, U.S. stock prices have not yet had time to catch up with the resurgence of inflation since the mid-1960s. An important characteristic of the early post–World War II period, however, not so far repeated in the post-1965 inflation, was an appreciable moderation of the inflation rate after the initial wartime episode.

The post–World War II experience suggests that, except for short-run fluctuations, stocks can maintain their real value over the very long run.[14] The past decade may be unusual because of the high valuation of equity per dollar of net worth attained in the mid-1960s. The onset of rapid inflation reduced the real rate of return and showed stocks to be vulnerable to increases in the rate of inflation. Given this uncertainty, the market value of equity earnings is likely to remain low. Even if the valuation remains low, however, a stable valuation would allow stocks to provide their historical role of a hedge against inflation, though at perhaps a lower than historical rate of return if inflation produces a less hospitable climate for business profits. Of course, whether stocks will in fact provide a hedge in the long run remains to be seen. If they do, they would meet the long-run purposes of pension funds and retirement savings. But the short-run instability of stocks makes their long-run reliability as a hedge against inflation uncertain until experience clarifies their long-run behavior in an inflationary environment.

Households

The unattractiveness of common stocks helps to explain household behavior which conflicts with the standard theory of the effects of inflation. For most households, saving is not easily rechanneled, but some response to changes in expected rates of return is likely to occur given sufficient time. From the onset of inflation in 1965 through 1972, household portfolios of financial assets at first did not change radically (Table 2-6). There was a slight rise in the share of equity holdings until 1968, reflecting the increase in stock prices rather than any net investment in equities by households. Households were purchasing investment fund shares while they were disinvesting in other equities at an even greater rate. After 1968 the share of equities dropped, especially after 1972, when the decline in stock prices, combined with continued net sales of equities by households, reduced equities from 39 to 22 percent of household financial assets. Deposits largely took the place of equities as an element of household assets.[15]

From a broader view of the household portfolio, which includes tangible assets such as land, owner-occupied housing, and consumer durables, it appears that a further shift took place after 1972—a reduction in the share of financial assets as a group and an increase in the share of tangible assets, from 37 to 47 percent (Table 2-7).[16] This suggests that households shifted from financial assets to real property and durable goods, as a theory of hedging against inflation would imply. The rise in housing wealth may mean that such a shift

Table 2-6. Distribution of Financial Assets of Households,[a] 1955-1977. (percent)

	Total	*Equity*[b] *(market value)*	*Market Instruments (par value)*			*Deposits*	*Deposits plus Short-term Market Instruments*	*Other*[d]
			Total	*Long- term*	*Short- term*[c]			
1955	100	40.5	16.6	8.7	7.9	24.3	32.2	18.7
1956	100	40.5	16.4	8.8	7.6	24.3	31.9	18.8
1957	100	36.1	17.4	9.5	7.9	26.2	34.1	20.4
1958	100	42.5	14.8	8.5	6.3	23.9	30.2	18.8
1959	100	42.5	14.9	8.8	6.1	23.7	29.8	18.8
1960	100	40.7	15.2	9.5	5.8	24.5	30.3	19.6
1961	100	44.9	13.7	8.6	5.1	22.8	28.0	18.6
1962	100	40.1	14.3	9.0	5.3	25.7	31.0	19.9
1963	100	42.1	13.4	8.5	5.0	25.1	30.1	19.3
1964	100	42.4	12.9	8.3	4.6	25.4	30.0	19.3
1965	100	43.4	12.0	7.5	4.6	25.5	30.1	19.1
1966	100	39.5	13.3	8.3	4.9	27.0	31.9	20.3
1967	100	43.2	11.6	7.4	4.2	25.9	30.1	19.3
1968	100	45.4	10.9	6.7	4.1	25.1	29.2	18.6
1969	100	40.6	12.9	8.0	4.9	26.5	31.4	20.0
1970	100	38.4	12.5	8.6	3.9	28.3	32.2	20.8
1971	100	39.2	11.1	8.1	3.0	28.9	31.9	20.8
1972	100	38.6	10.6	7.8	2.8	29.7	32.4	21.1
1973	100	29.8	12.6	8.8	3.8	35.2	39.0	22.4
1974	100	20.4	15.4	10.6	4.8	40.4	45.1	23.8
1975	100	23.2	14.4	10.0	4.4	38.7	43.1	23.7
1976	100	25.4	13.1	9.5	3.6	38.0	41.6	23.5
1977	100	21.7	13.2	9.1	4.1	40.6	44.7	24.5

Source: *Flow of Funds Accounts, 1946-1975* (December 1976) for 1955-1971; 1972-1977 data directly from Federal Reserve Board, tables on Financial Assets and Liabilities: Households, Personal Trusts, and Nonprofit Organizations.

Note: Total is sum of columns in boldface.

[a]Includes personal trusts and nonprofit organizations.

[b]Includes investment company shares.

[c]Includes savings bonds, short-term marketable Treasury securities, open market paper, and money market fund shares.

[d]Includes life insurance and pension fund reserves, security credit, and miscellaneous assets.

Table 2-7. Tangible and Financial Assets of Households, 1955-1977. (billions of 1964 dollars)

	Total	Owner-Occupied Housing	Land	Consumer Durables	Financial Assets[a]	Percent of Total Financial	Percent of Total All Tangible
1955	1,343.6	258.7	98.8	162.3	823.8	61.3	38.7
1956	1,402.5	270.4	110.1	169.0	853.0	60.8	39.2
1957	1,388.3	280.3	119.6	174.0	814.3	58.7	41.3
1958	1,551.8	297.3	131.6	175.1	947.8	61.1	38.9
1959	1,650.0	315.8	148.9	179.2	1,005.8	61.0	39.0
1960	1,683.1	326.7	155.8	181.8	1,018.9	60.5	39.5
1961	1,851.1	336.9	168.6	183.6	1,162.0	62.8	37.2
1962	1,834.0	345.8	177.8	188.1	1,122.2	61.2	38.8
1963	1,971.9	356.0	187.0	194.3	1,234.6	62.6	37.4
1964	2,100.0	368.0	198.0	203.5	1,330.5	63.4	36.6
1965	2,237.0	375.0	208.7	215.6	1,437.7	64.3	35.7
1966	2,200.8	375.8	213.1	227.8	1,384.1	62.9	37.1
1967	2,413.7	395.7	219.0	240.8	1,558.2	64.6	35.4
1968	2,589.7	431.0	220.7	254.3	1,683.7	65.0	35.0
1969	2,476.7	444.5	227.7	262.6	1,541.9	62.3	37.7
1970	2,446.3	442.1	226.4	266.7	1,511.1	61.8	38.2
1971	2,602.1	455.7	233.4	278.2	1,634.8	62.8	37.2
1972	2,787.6	492.1	252.0	293.8	1,749.8	62.8	37.2
1973	2,605.8	522.3	267.5	302.5	1,513.5	58.1	41.9
1974	2,362.8	524.8	268.8	300.3	1,268.9	53.7	46.3
1975	2,496.3	538.3	278.1	307.9	1,372.0	55.0	45.0
1976	2,694.2	579.8	296.9	320.2	1,497.2	55.6	44.4
1977	2,709.7	621.7	318.3	323.9	1,445.8	53.4	46.6

Sources: Financial assets from *Flow of Funds Accounts, 1946-1975* (December 1976) for 1955-1971; 1972-1977 data directly from Federal Reserve Board, tables on Financial Assets and Liabilities: Households, Personal Trusts, and Nonprofit Organizations. Bureau of Economic Analysis for tangible assets except land. Land is from Raymond Goldsmith's worksheets for the National Bureau's project on The Measurement of Economic and Social Performance. Land values were extrapolated for 1976-1977 by the value of owner-occupied housing.
   Dollar figures deflated by year end CPI, all items.

[a]Includes financial assets of personal trusts and nonprofit organizations. All except common stock are at face value.

was desired, but the fact that the increase arose from capital gains in tangible assets, rather than from net purchases, casts doubt on the interpretation of deliberate hedging. Table 2-8, which presents ratios of household asset acquisition to personal disposable income, shows that the increase in total asset acquisition between 1955-1964 and 1965-1974 was largely in financial assets, only a small part of which was contractual saving through pension funds. Households did not invest more in real assets as a hedge when inflation acceler-

Table 2-8. Asset Acquisition of Households as percent of Personal Disposable Income, 1955-1977.

		Tangible Assets			Financial Assets[a]			
	Total	Total	Residential Housing	Consumer Durables	Total Net	Equity	Pension Fund Reserves	Other Net
1955	11.7	10.1	5.9	4.2	1.7	0.3	2.0	−0.6
1956	12.0	8.1	5.3	2.8	3.8	0.7	2.1	1.0
1957	11.3	6.8	4.3	2.5	4.5	0.5	2.2	1.8
1958	10.0	5.0	3.9	1.1	5.0	0.5	2.3	2.2
1959	10.6	6.9	4.5	2.4	3.7	0.2	2.5	1.0
1960	9.4	6.1	4.0	2.1	3.3	−0.2	2.4	1.1
1961	9.0	4.7	3.4	1.3	4.3	0.1	2.4	1.8
1962	9.8	5.6	3.2	2.4	4.3	−0.5	2.3	2.5
1963	10.6	6.3	3.3	3.0	4.3	−0.6	2.4	2.5
1964	12.0	6.5	3.1	3.5	5.4	0	2.6	2.8
1965	12.4	6.8	2.8	4.0	5.6	−0.4	2.5	3.5
1966	13.2	6.4	2.3	4.1	6.8	−0.1	2.8	4.1
1967	12.8	5.6	2.2	3.4	7.2	−0.8	2.5	5.5
1968	12.6	6.4	2.3	4.1	6.2	−1.1	2.6	4.7
1969	10.3	5.9	2.2	3.7	4.4	−0.7	2.5	2.6
1970	11.8	4.3	1.8	2.5	7.5	−0.1	2.8	4.8
1971	13.3	5.8	2.5	3.3	7.5	−0.5	2.8	5.2
1972	13.7	7.3	3.2	4.1	6.4	−0.6	2.8	4.2
1973	14.6	7.4	3.1	4.3	7.2	−0.8	2.8	5.2
1974	12.6	5.0	2.3	2.7	7.6	−0.2	3.0	4.8
1975	12.9	4.0	1.9	2.1	8.9	−0.4	3.4	5.6
1976	12.3	6.2	2.7	3.5	6.1	−0.3	3.9	2.5
1977	11.4	7.1	3.6	3.5	4.3	−0.1	4.3	0.1
Averages								
1955-1964	10.6	6.6	4.1	2.5	4.0	0.1	2.3	1.6
1965-1974	12.7	6.1	2.5	3.6	6.6	−0.5	2.7	4.5
1975-1977	12.2	5.8	2.7	3.0	6.4	−0.3	3.9	2.7

Note: Investment in tangible assets is net of depreciation. Personal disposable income is adjusted to include government insurance credits and capital gains dividends. Tangible assets exclude investment by nonprofit organizations. Totals may not equal sum of components because of rounding.

Source: *Flow of Funds Accounts, 1946-1975* (December 1976), for 1955-1973; *Flow of Funds Accounts, 4th Quarter 1977* (February 1978), for 1974-1977, table on Saving and Investment: Households, Personal Trusts, and Nonprofit Organizations.

[a]Includes personal trusts and nonprofit organizations.

ated in 1965. In fact, they tended to reduce the share of income devoted to acquisitions of housing and common stock, assets that might have been expected to be the object of inflation-induced saving. There was, however, some increase in investment in consumer durables.

The savings ratios in Table 2-9 show that not only asset acquisitions

Table 2-9. Forms of Household Saving as Percent of Personal Disposable Income, 1955-1977.

				N e t	*S a v i n g*			
		Total			*T h r o u g h*			
	NIA Basis (2)+(7)	*FOF Basis (3)+(4)*	*Tangible Assets*	*Financial Assets and Liabilities (5)+(6)*	*Finan-cial Assets*	*Lia-bilities*	*Discrep-ancy*
	(1)	*(2)*	*(3)*	*(4)*	*(5)*	*(6)*	*(7)*
1955	9.9	11.7	10.1	1.7	9.0	−7.3	−1.8
1956	10.1	12.0	8.1	3.8	9.4	−5.6	−1.9
1957	9.5	11.3	6.8	4.5	8.6	−4.1	−1.8
1958	8.3	10.0	5.0	5.0	9.2	−4.2	−1.7
1959	8.5	10.6	6.9	3.7	10.1	−6.5	−2.1
1960	7.5	9.4	6.1	3.3	8.6	−5.3	−1.9
1961	7.4	9.0	4.7	4.3	9.4	−5.1	−1.6
1962	8.0	9.8	5.6	4.3	9.9	−5.7	−1.8
1963	8.1	10.6	6.3	4.3	11.4	−7.1	−2.5
1964	10.0	12.0	6.5	5.4	12.1	−6.7	−2.0
1965	10.9	12.4	6.8	5.6	12.2	−6.6	−1.5
1966	11.2	13.2	6.4	6.8	11.4	−4.6	−2.0
1967	11.6	12.7	5.6	7.2	12.0	−4.8	−1.1
1968	11.5	12.6	6.4	6.2	12.2	−6.0	−1.1
1969	10.3	10.2	5.9	4.4	9.2	−4.9	0.1
1970	10.9	11.8	4.3	7.5	11.0	−3.5	−0.9
1971	12.0	13.3	5.8	7.5	13.5	−6.0	−1.3
1972	11.5	13.7	7.3	6.4	15.0	−8.6	−2.2
1973	13.1	14.5	7.4	7.2	14.9	−7.7	−1.4
1974	11.1	12.7	5.0	7.6	12.5	−4.9	−1.6
1975	10.6	12.9	4.0	8.9	13.6	−4.7	−2.3
1976	10.5	12.3	6.2	6.1	14.0	−8.0	−1.8
1977	10.1	11.4	7.1	4.3	14.5	−10.2	−1.3
Averages							
1955-1964	8.7	10.6	6.6	4.0	9.7	−5.8	−1.9
1965-1974	11.4	14.1	6.1	6.6	12.4	−5.8	−1.3
1975-1977	10.4	12.2	5.8	6.4	14.0	−7.6	−1.8

Source: *Flow of Funds Accounts, 1946-1975* (December 1976) for 1955-1973; *Flow of Funds Accounts, 4th Quarter 1977* (February 1978) for 1974-1977, tables on Saving and Investment: Households, Personal Trusts, and Nonprofit Organizations. Savings on NIA basis are adjusted to *Flow of Funds Accounts* concepts by adding credits from government insurance, capital gains dividends, and net durables in consumption.

but also total saving rates, calculated from either Flow of Funds or National Income and Product Accounts, were at a high level in the decade after 1965. There was no move toward more rapid acquisition of liabilities, relative to income, as might be expected if households were attempting to speculate on a high rate of inflation. Thus, households were not clearly avoiding financial assets or seeking financial liabilities as a result of the acceleration of inflation.

The shift of household wealth from financial assets to housing reflects the fact that residential property values have continued to climb faster than general prices (Table 2-10) and that financial assets have depreciated in real terms (even though we do not calculate the additional depreciation from the rise in interest rates). It could be that there was a shift in household demand to housing assets but that it had the result mainly of raising their prices, since

Table 2-10. Indicators of Single-Family Home Prices, 1963-1977. (1966=100)

	Nominal (Dollar) Prices			Deflated Prices		
	New Single-Family Homes		Existing Single-Family Homes Median Sales Price	New Single-Family Homes		Existing Single-Family Homes Median Sales Price
	Price Index[a]	Average Sales Price		Price Index[a]	Average Sales Price	
1963	93.4	84.1		99.0	89.1	
1964	94.3	88.3		98.7	92.4	
1965	96.5	93.5		99.5	96.4	
1966	100.0	100.0	100.0	100.0	100.0	100.0
1967	103.5	106.1	104.6	100.7	103.2	101.8
1968	108.8	115.4	113.8	101.6	107.8	106.3
1969	117.6	119.6	119.7	104.2	106.0	106.1
1970	121.5	109.3	124.3	101.6	91.4	104.0
1971	127.5	117.8	135.5	102.3	94.5	108.7
1972	135.6	129.0	147.4	105.3	100.2	114.5
1973	149.9	151.9	160.5	109.6	111.0	117.3
1974	163.7	167.8	177.9	107.8	110.5	117.2
1975	180.4	183.6	194.8	108.9	110.8	117.6
1976	198.1	206.5	212.2	113.0	117.8	121.1
1977	215.7	227.1	240.5	115.6	121.7	128.9

Source: New single-family homes—Price index: U.S. Bureau of the Census, Construction Reports: C27-77-Q1, June 1977, for 1963-1976. 1977 figure extrapolated from first three quarters, C27-77-03, December 1977.

New single-family homes—Average prices: U.S. Bureau of the Census, Construction Reports: C25 75-12, March 1976, for 1963-1972; C26-77-5, July 1977, for 1973-1976; C26-77-12, February 1978, for 1977.

Existing single-family homes—Median prices: December sales, National Association of Real Estate Boards, Annual Report 1975, 1976, 1977.

Deflation by CPI, annual average.

[a]Price index for single-family house identical to average house sold in 1967, with respect to eight characteristics.

the current output of housing is small relative to the stock, and there is no current output of land. The rise in prices may have achieved a desired increase in the share of tangible assets in total wealth. But did the demand for real assets increase, or did households simply benefit unexpectedly from the rising relative cost of residential construction and relative scarcity of land with growth in the population?

A possible indication of the attitudes of households is that the value-to-debt ratio for owner-occupied housing did not increase by the full amount of the rise in housing values due to inflation. Households liquidated part of the capital gains on housing by borrowing on existing homes, or as shown by Table 2-11, by borrowing on new and existing homes in excess of the net investment in them, particularly since 1971. The ratio of market value to debt of homes rose because the price increase outran the increase in debt, but the rise in the ratio was small considering the size of the rise in home prices. The borrowing is presumably due to a desire to "cash in," facilitated by a high rate of turnover of existing homes. Such borrowing is equivalent to selling part of the equity in residential property and reducing the amount by which it serves as a hedge against the uncertainty of inflation rates. But the borrowing would not be undertaken to satisfy a desire to hedge, except to the extent that the funds were used to invest in other real property or education. To the contrary, borrowing is a speculation that future inflation rates will be higher than the compensation for inflation built into prevailing mortgage rates; its attractiveness may reflect the fact that mortgaged houses are virtually the only medium for such speculation available to most households. Although the escalation of inflation in 1965 made real property more attractive as an investment, it did not therefore materially affect the net acquisition rate, in part because most households need to borrow to buy property and because borrowing costs at least partly reflected expected rates of inflation.

Households have clearly not tried to use corporate equity as a hedge against inflation in recent years. They have accumulated real property as a hedge, but largely by passively accepting the rise in its price and in its consequent share of household assets rather than by acquiring new real estate assets. Overall, total saving has increased via financial assets, as Table 2-9 showed.

How is an increase in household saving largely in the form of fixed-dollar assets to be explained during a period of rising inflation? One answer is that households wanted to restore financial assets unexpectedly depreciated by inflation. In real terms total household financial assets, as shown in Table 2-7, hardly increased

Table 2-11. Household Saving Through Owner-Occupied Housing, 1955–1977. (billions of 1964 dollars)

	Net Investment in Housing (1)	Net Borrowing on Home Mortgages (2)	Net Saving in Housing (3)	Capital Gains in Housing (4)
1955	18.7	13.6	5.1	14.6
1956	17.7	12.8	4.9	8.7
1957	14.7	9.9	4.8	8.6
1958	13.4	10.5	2.9	15.8
1959	16.4	13.2	3.2	15.0
1960	14.8	12.1	2.7	5.0
1961	13.0	13.1	−0.1	10.1
1962	12.9	14.3	−1.4	7.7
1963	13.8	16.6	−2.8	9.1
1964	13.6	17.2	−3.6	11.2
1965	13.3	16.8	−3.5	7.2
1966	11.5	12.8	−1.3	4.6
1967	11.1	12.5	−1.4	22.7
1968	12.4	15.0	−2.6	36.1
1969	11.7	15.4	−3.7	23.4
1970	9.9	11.8	−1.9	4.6
1971	14.5	20.8	−6.3	13.6
1972	19.2	30.8	−11.6	39.0
1973	19.5	32.8	−13.3	54.7
1974	14.5	22.3	−7.8	26.9
1975	11.9	21.9	−10.0	25.9
1976	17.9	33.4	−15.5	36.5
1977	24.8	44.5	−19.7	41.1
Averages				
1955-1964	14.9	13.3	1.6	10.6
1965-1974	13.8	19.1	−5.3	23.3
1975-1977	18.2	33.3	−15.1	34.5

Sources:

Column (1): Residential construction, including mobile homes, less capital consumption on housing. *Flow of Funds Accounts, 1946-1975* (December 1976) for 1955-1973; *Flow of Funds Accounts, 4th Quarter 1977* (February 1978) for 1974-1977, table on Saving and Investment: Households, Personal Trusts, and Nonprofit Organizations.

Column (2): *Flow of Funds Accounts,* same as column (1).

Column (3): Column (1) minus column (2).

Column (4): For structures, the difference between changes in current cost and changes in historical cost, in 1964 dollars. For land, calculated as in Table 2-2, column (7).

Dollar figures deflated: all flows by annual average CPI; capital stock by end-of-year CPI.

after 1968, and by 1974 and 1975, they were below the level of the late 1960s. Since many econometric studies of saving find that wealth and saving are inversely related, other things being equal, the decline in wealth helps to explain the increase in saving rates in the period after 1968.

How large could the inflation-induced wealth effect on saving be? Studies of personal saving or consumption suggest that the wealth effect is on the order of 5 percent or less of changes in wealth.[17] To put this in perspective, the net financial wealth of households was about two-and-a-half times personal disposable income in 1965. A rise in the inflation rate would reduce real wealth by the full amount of the higher rate of price increase only if the higher rate were unanticipated and if it were not accompanied by offsetting adjustments in interest rates and equity prices. An unanticipated rise in prices of 4 percent, say, assuming no offsetting adjustments, would reduce real wealth by the same percentage and increase saving at most by $(0.04 \times 0.05 \times 2.5 =)$ 0.5 percent of income.

The inability to meet the uncertainty of inflation through satisfactory hedges may itself have also contributed to increased saving. A study by Taylor [1974][18] finds that total as well as financial saving varies positively with the inflation rate, *when the effect of wealth is held constant.* A plausible interpretation of this result is that higher inflation increases uncertainty about the fuure value of assets and real income and that households save more, as they typically do, in response to an uncertain income stream. The fact that households increased financial saving, primarily through the acquisition of fixed-dollar liquid assets, is consistent with a desire to increase liquidity in the face of uncertainty. This desire helps to explain the anomaly during inflation, so far as the standard theory of its effects is concerned, of household additions to holdings of the very assets that are subject to depreciation in purchasing power by inflation.

Taylor also analyzed a cross-section sample of households to see whether they hedged against the uncertainty of inflation by acquiring real estate. One of his variables identified respondents who were so uncertain about the rate of inflation that they would not offer a prediction. This variable had a *negative* effect on household purchases of real property and common stocks, except for a positive effect on the real property purchases of high-wealth households. These estimates do not have high reliability, but they are roughly consistent with other indications that inflation has not led to greater household purchases of real assets and equity.

Interest rates rose rapidly beginning in 1965, and rates on fixed-dollar assets eventually compensated for a good part of the actual rate of inflation and, perhaps, for all of the anticipated rate. Once this rise had occurred, households had no incentive to avoid fixed-dollar assets unless they sought a hedge against inflation rates that might go higher than was expected. Flows increased into savings deposits, even though at times they paid far less than did market instruments (represented in Figure 2-3 by the commercial paper rate). An attraction of deposits, was that they were safe from the risk attached to market securities of a decline in nominal value should interest rates rise further, though deposits shared with all financial assets the loss in real value from inflation itself. Thus deposits, as well as other short-term assets, were presumably acquired as a form of a hedge against interest rate uncertainty despite their lack of inflation protection.

At first sight, it might seem that continuing strong flows into low-paying deposits and other fixed-dollar assets at a time of inflationary resurgence meant that households were not sensitive to differences in rates of return. This presumption, however, is contradicted by the events of several recent periods. There were sharp reductions of inflows into mutual savings banks and savings and loan associations in 1966, 1969, and 1973–1974 from a steeply rising trend when

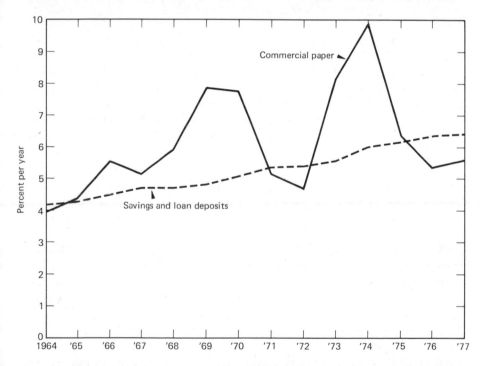

Source: Prime commercial paper, four to six months, *Annual Report of the Council of Economic Advisers*; average rate paid on savings deposits of savings and loan associations, United States League of Savings Associations, *Savings and Loan Fact Book.*

Figure 2-3. Interest rates on Savings Deposits and Commercial Paper, 1964–77

open market rates shot well above the ceiling rates on deposits of those institutions. There was a rise in loans on life insurance policies in the late 1960s when they offered contractual loans at a 5 percent rate, well below other alternatives. Both demonstrated the public's responsiveness to interest rate differentials (see Table 2-12). Also, econometric studies of portfolio decisions have long found interest rates to be significant.[19] In addition to portfolio allocations, some recent research by Boskin [1978] indicates that aggregate saving increases with a rise in interest rates, despite the inability of earlier studies to find such a relation.

As an alternative explanation of the deposit flows, it might be thought that households did not anticipate inflation. The study by Taylor [1974] cited earlier contains an analysis of a cross-section of households which bears on this question. He found that the typical expected rates of inflation among the households in the samples were quite close to actual rates. Moreover, if failure to anticipate inflation were important, households that did anticipate it and those that did not would reveal differences in saving behavior. Based on the financial condition of a sample of households in 1959 and in 1967 and their expectations of inflation, Taylor found no systematic relation between reported expectations of inflation and the acquisition of various kinds of assets. This was true of households standardized for income, wealth, and demographic characteristics. These data pertain to the period before 1968 when the market value of common stocks had been rising and appeared to be keeping up with inflation, and households might therefore have considered them an appropriate source of protection. Taylor's findings suggest that the absence of major portfolio adjustments does not reflect failure to anticipate inflation.

It would not be valid to conclude that the reason household portfolios did not change was that anticipated inflation had no effect on household behavior. For, in that event, we should have no explanation for the substantial rise in interest rates since 1965. The explanation therefore seems to be that the rise in nominal interest rates was sufficient to forestall major shifts in household portfolios. The rise in interest rates produced unanticipated capital losses on bonds, but thereafter yields were sufficient to compensate for anticipated inflation, and households maintained their fixed-dollar holdings. Since households generally do not invest heavily in market instruments, they continued to acquire depository assets, except in certain periods when the differentials became unusually wide. The importance of the uncertainty of inflation in producing a desire for greater liquidity seems to be the only plausible explanation.

Table 2-12. Financial Saving of Households, 1965-1977. (billions of dollars)

		Through Financial Intermediaries						Direct					
	Total	Total	Com-mercial Banks	Savings Insti-tutions	Invest-ment Company Shares^a	Life Insurance Reserves^b	Pension Fund Reserves	Total	Federal and Municipal Securities	Cor-porate and Foreign Bonds	Com-mercial Paper	Mort-gages	Cor-porate Equities
1965	54.6	55.1	22.3	13.1	3.3	4.3	12.1	−0.5	4.0	0.5	*	0.4	−5.4
1966	**55.7**	**43.0**	**14.3**	**7.2**	**3.7**	**3.3**	**14.5**	**12.7**	**11.0**	**1.4**	**2.7**	**2.0**	**−4.4**
1967	62.2	66.2	28.4	16.6	3.0	4.2	14.0	−4.0	−0.6	4.0	−2.2	2.1	−7.3
1968	66.6	66.9	29.0	13.0	5.9	3.4	15.6	−0.3	5.6	4.2	−0.5	2.8	−12.4
1969	**57.2**	**35.3**	**3.2**	**8.4**	**4.9**	**2.5**	**16.3**	**21.9**	**19.9**	**5.4**	**3.8**	**2.2**	**−9.4**
1970	72.7	77.1	35.5	16.6	2.8	3.0	19.2	−4.4	−9.0	9.5	−3.2	1.8	−3.5
1971	98.2	104.1	36.9	39.6	1.3	5.2	21.1	−5.9	−10.8	8.3	0.3	1.3	−5.0
1972	121.6	113.3	40.1	45.4	−0.5	5.7	22.6	8.3	1.7	4.2	*	6.4	−4.0
1973	**135.6**	**109.9**	**52.0**	**28.4**	**−1.2**	**5.1**	**25.6**	**25.7**	**23.5**	**0.9**	**3.4**	**3.6**	**−5.7**
1974	**133.9**	**98.1**	**41.2**	**21.8**	**1.7**	**3.8**	**29.6**	**35.8**	**22.6**	**4.7**	**5.7**	**4.3**	**−1.5**
1975	156.1	134.2	32.4	59.4	1.2	3.8	37.4	21.9	20.7	8.2	−6.0	2.9	−3.9
1976	180.4	167.7	47.6	69.1	−1.2	5.6	46.6	12.7	3.2	4.0	−0.2	8.6	−2.9
1977	209.9	187.7	56.1	69.7	−1.4	6.3	57.0	22.2	11.7	0.2	−1.5	11.3	0.5

Note: Investment in noncorporate business and miscellaneous assets not shown. Years of credit market stringency shown in bold face.

Source: *Flow of Funds Accounts, 1946-1975* (December 1976) for 1965-1973; *Flow of Funds Accounts, 4th Quarter 1977* (February 1978) for 1974-1977, table on Saving and Investment: Household, Personal Trusts, and Nonprofit Organizations.

^aIncludes money market funds.
^bNet of policy loans.
*Less than 0.05 billion.

Additional evidence has been provided by Wachtel [1977][20] in a time series study which estimates the separate influences on saving of interest rates and households' uncertainty about future inflation rates. The measure of inflation uncertainty, which differs from Taylor's, is the average variance of inflationary expectations across households. Wachtel's results confirm the indications of other studies that uncertainty increases saving, suggesting that this effect is probably the main explanation for the observed rise in saving when inflation accelerates. In analyzing the components of saving, he found that the main channel of the uncertainty effect on saving is through a reduction in consumer credit, suggesting that households prepare for an uncertain future by avoiding financial commitments.

In contrast to the standard theory, therefore, in which an acceleration of inflation leads to an initial shift from financial saving to equity and real property and to increased indebtedness, and to some degree to a permanent shift for purposes of hedging, the recent behavior of households under inflation differed materially. Households saved a larger fraction of income and channeled little of it into equities, with almost all financial saving going into fixed-dollar assets. Part of this represented a restoration of the share of wealth held in fixed-dollar form, which was most eroded by inflation. But that is hardly the full explanation. From all indications, this behavior also reflected a desire for greater liquidity in the face of uncertainty over how high inflation rates might go.

It is conceivable that, after a period of adjustment, if the volatility of inflation moderates and anticipations of the rate of inflation prove reasonably accurate, common stocks may keep pace with the rate of inflation over the long run and provide a hedge against moderate departures from the anticipated average rate. In this situation, also, saving would presumably settle down to a normal level. If the current inflation does not accelerate further in the next few years, we shall have a test of saving behavior under conditions of stable inflation.

In any event, it is hard to see the current situation continuing. Real rates of interest on deposits, at current inflation rates, are around zero or negative. But we have no insight as to whether the next development will be an abatement of inflation or a further rise in interest rates.

While the effects of inflation on the household sector as a whole are of primary importance for financial institutions and markets, differences among households in the impact of inflation are of concern for questions of equity and burden. We expect such differences partly because households differ in the composition of their assets and liabilities, though there are also many other factors, such as changes in current income and living costs, that determine the effect of inflation on individual households.

Two elements enter the calculation of effects on household balance sheets. One is the composition of the balance sheet: the type of assets held and the degree to which they are leveraged by debt. The second is the behavior of various assets' prices during inflation.

In a study of the 1950s, a period of mild inflation compared with recent experience, Goldsmith and Lipsey calculated leverage ratios and asset price changes for various groups of households[21] and found that leverage ratios did not differ widely by wealth, income, or occupation, but did show a consistent pattern by age, generally declining with age of head from the peak level in the twenty-five to thirty-four age group. The main differences were for consumer capital assets (housing and consumer durable equipment), where the oldest families had ratios perhaps half that of the peak group. Only in the twenty-five to thirty-four age group was the leverage ratio above one. We may interpret these ratios as indicating that, if all age groups held the same price-sensitive assets, only the twenty-five to thirty-four age group would enjoy a gain in net worth that exceeded the gain in asset prices. The older the families, the more their real net worth would be reduced by inflation. The main reason for the differences was that the twenty-five to thirty-four age group was most likely to have both price-sensitive assets (a home) and a large debt (a mortgage).

The change in price for price-sensitive assets differed among wealth groups in the 1950s, with higher wealth being associated with larger price gains, except for the highest wealth group (gross estates of $10 million and over). The reason was that the proportion of common stock in price-sensitive assets was positively related to wealth and that stock prices outdistanced other prices during these years. The top wealth group, however, did not have such large stockholdings, probably because they substituted tax-exempt bonds for common stocks.

The characteristic of families that strongly distinguished between those likely to gain from inflation and those likely to lose was their homeownership status. Homeowners with mortgages, as a group, had a leverage ratio of 1.15, homeowners without mortgages a ratio of 0.78, and renters a ratio of 0.58. The implication of these ratios is that a rise in price of price-sensitive assets equal to the rate of inflation would have produced a 15 percent increase in real net worth for homeowners with mortgages, while renters would have suffered a loss of 42 percent in real net worth. The rankings of the three housing-status groups were the same for virtually all income, age, and occupation groups. The highest leverage ratios, around 1.5, were those of young families owning mortgaged homes; and the ratio fell sharply with age, presumably reflecting lower mortgage-to-value ratios among older homeowners who had been paying off their mortgages for some time.

The effect of inflation on net worth for any group reflects also the rate of increase in asset prices. The range of asset price changes was not very large from 1949 to 1958 among income or wealth classes in the two homeowner groups, but among renters there were high price increases among those with the highest incomes, the oldest age group (sixty-five and over), and the retired. The reason was that these groups had high proportions of common stock among their price-sensitive assets during a period of large gains in stock prices.

If we combine the leverage ratios and the asset prices, we can estimate the changes in real net worth that would have occurred in the absence of saving or trading of assets. Half of the groups of renters would have had declines in real net worth betwen 1949 and 1958, despite the rise in stock prices; most groups of homeowners without mortgages, small positive changes; and most groups of owners of mortgaged homes, gains of over 10 percent.

No similar analysis has been performed for the period since 1965, but the main relationships must have been the same, except for the absence of the stock price rise that aided wealthier, older, and retired groups, particularly renters, in the 1950s. Therefore, the result of the recent inflation must have been losses in real net worth for almost all groups of renters; small gains for homeowners without mortgages and those with small mortgages, since house prices again outpaced the general price level; and substantial gains for heavily mortgaged homeowners, mostly young families.

For the household sector as a whole, therefore, real property values have withstood inflation, but financial assets, including equity, have been eroded in real terms. Despite this outcome, households have continued to invest heavily in fixed-dollar assets because of the limitations of real property and the safety of deposits and short-term assets.

Financial Intermediaries

The development once thought to be the main danger to financial intermediaries from inflation—that households would shun fixed-dollar assets and thus reduce the inflow of funds—has not materialized. Nevertheless, intermediaries have suffered from the unprecedented changes in interest rates which have resulted both from inflation and from efforts to halt inflation. The problem has been particularly acute where legal or contractual limitations have prevented or slowed the response of intermediaries to the rise in market rates of interest.

In the long run, after their interest rates have risen to compensate for anticipated inflation, intermediaries are able to pay a rate on their liabilities that maintains their competitive position in the financial structure. But, in the short run, some intermediaries have encountered difficult problems in the changing inflationary environment. Because their asset holdings are mostly long term, intermediaries responding to competitive pressures to pay higher rates on their liabilities are hampered by average rates of return on their portfolios that rise more slowly than market interest rates. The transition is not short, since it requires a turnover of a large portion of the loans and securities in their portfolios acquired earlier at lower rates. Transitional pressures underlay most of the difficulties the intermediaries underwent in recent periods of monetary restraint when short-term market rates rose sharply and the intermediaries faced massive reductions in the inflow of funds.

The buffetings taken by financial intermediaries are highlighted in Table 2-13, which shows sharp declines in the amount and share of total lending in 1966, 1969, and 1974—periods of sharply rising interest rates, when investors bypassed the intermediaries to invest directly in market securities. Public agencies also increased their lending in credit markets directly in 1974. In all three episodes, disintermediation occurred—that is, a decline not only in the share of intermediaries but also in the absolute amount of funds supplied by them. Given the rate of inflation, the decreases in real terms were even larger than those shown in current dollars.

Accompanying the abrupt shifts to and from direct financing were substantial changes in the shares of the major institutions in the part of total financing that was done through financial intermediaries (Table 2-14). Between 1965 and 1977, the share of commercial banks ranged from 23 to 57 percent, that of savings institutions from 17 to 43 percent, and that of insurance and pension funds from 12 to 36 percent. The commercial banks were sharply affected by the money market tightness in 1966 and 1969. Within the insurance and pension fund sector, there was some shift away from life insurance companies, particularly in the early 1970s and, for the life companies, a considerable substitution of pension reserves for life insurance reserves as a source of funds. The comparatively slow growth of the life insurance business, which offers long-term investments fixed in monetary terms, is surely not unrelated to the inflationary environment of the past decade.

Table 2-13. Sources of Funds Advanced to Nonfinancial Sectors, 1955-1977. (billions of dollars)

	Total Funds Raised by Nonfinancial Sectors	Funds Advanced by					Private Financial Intermediaries as Percent of	
		Public Agencies and Foreign Net[a]	Private Domestic Nonfinancial Investors		Private Financial Intermediaries		Total	Total Private Domestic
			Equity[b]	Direct Lending	Equity[c]	Direct Lending[d]		
1955	37.9	1.4	0.3	14.0	1.6	20.5	58.3	60.5
1956	29.8	2.3	1.2	3.8	1.2	21.4	75.8	82.2
1957	30.6	0.6	0.6	5.7	1.9	21.8	77.5	79.0
1958	42.2	3.9	-0.1	2.6	2.4	33.4	84.8	93.5
1959	52.9	4.9	-0.8	20.8	3.1	24.9	52.9	58.3
1960	38.6	3.5	-1.8	3.3	3.3	30.3	87.0	95.7
1961	47.7	4.0	-1.5	4.3	3.9	36.9	85.5	93.4
1962	54.7	5.4	-3.7	4.5	4.0	44.4	88.4	98.2
1963	59.4	5.2	-3.7	10.6	3.5	43.8	79.6	87.3
1964	69.3	7.3	-2.5	8.2	3.9	52.5	81.4	91.0
1965	71.7	6.9	-5.8	9.4	6.1	55.1	85.4	94.4
1966	**69.3**	7.3	-4.7	17.4	5.7	43.6	**71.7**	79.5
1967	83.9	11.9	-6.5	4.8	9.1	64.6	87.8	102.4
1968	98.4	9.0	-10.3	20.6	9.1	68.8	81.2	89.4
1969	**93.7**	6.8	-7.0	45.0	10.7	38.0	**53.0**	57.2
1970	100.6	19.6	-3.7	-0.1	10.9	75.4	83.6	104.8
1971	153.5	37.5	-5.6	0.3	9.5	104.3	78.2	104.6
1972	177.8	11.4	-1.6	23.3	17.0	132.6	81.4	87.2
1973	**202.0**	14.2	**-2.9**	45.5	12.5	134.7	**71.9**	**77.2**
1974	**189.6**	**29.6**	**-0.9**	**45.9**	**5.0**	**110.3**	**60.7**	**72.1**
1975	205.6	30.8	0.7	45.3	9.5	119.5	62.6	73.8
1976	268.3	36.0	-0.1	43.7	10.6	178.1	70.3	81.2
1977	335.9	58.5	3.1	62.9	8.4	206.1	63.9	77.3
Averages								
1955-1964	46.3	3.8	-1.2	7.8	2.9	33.0	77.5	84.5
1965-1974	124.0	15.4	-4.9	21.2	9.7	82.8	74.6	85.2
1975-1977	269.9	41.8	1.2	50.6	9.5	167.9	65.7	77.8

Source: *Flow of Funds Accounts, 1946-1975* (December 1976) for 1955-1966; *Flow of Funds Accounts, 3rd Quarter 1977* (November 1977), and *Flow of Funds Accounts, 4th Quarter 1977* (February 1978) for 1967-1977, tables on Funds Raised in Credit Markets and Credit Market Supply of Funds.

Note: Years of credit market stringency shown in bold face.

[a] Excluding agency borrowing and pool security issues.

[b] "Other net purchases" of corporate equities less net issues of mutual fund shares, assumed to be purchased by nonfinancial sectors.

[c] Corporate equity funds raised by private nonfinancial sectors less funds advanced by private domestic nonfinancial sectors.

[d] Total credit market funds advanced less credit market borrowing.

Table 2-14. Shares of Institutions in Credit Market Funds Advanced by Private Financial Institutions, 1955-1977. (percent)

| | | | | Insurance and Pension Funds | | |
| | | | | | of which Life | |
	Total	Commercial Banking	Savings Institutions	Total	Insurance Companies	Other Finance
1955	100	18.0	32.8	34.0	20.5	15.2
1956	100	24.8	33.4	38.1	23.5	3.6
1957	100	22.0	31.4	38.5	21.1	8.1
1958	100	45.5	27.3	27.8	15.3	−0.6
1959	100	16.7	36.1	34.1	17.3	13.1
1960	100	27.8	28.9	29.8	15.4	13.4
1961	100	39.7	31.0	26.0	13.8	3.2
1962	100	39.7	29.3	23.6	12.5	7.4
1963	100	34.8	35.1	23.1	12.9	7.0
1964	100	40.2	28.2	22.4	12.1	9.2
1965	100	46.3	23.2	21.8	12.3	8.6
1966	100	37.5	17.0	35.7	17.3	9.8
1967	100	56.6	23.6	20.4	11.7	−0.5
1968	100	51.2	20.4	18.3	9.7	10.0
1969	100	32.5	25.5	23.2	12.1	18.8
1970	100	45.3	22.6	22.3	9.1	9.7
1971	100	46.0	35.7	13.0	7.4	5.4
1972	100	47.2	31.6	11.9	6.5	9.2
1973	100	52.8	22.0	14.6	7.5	10.6
1974	100	51.1	21.3	23.8	10.2	3.7
1975	100	23.0	43.4	34.6	14.1	−0.9
1976	100	31.0	38.3	25.4	12.7	5.3
1977	100	32.9	35.6	25.2	11.1	6.4
Averages						
1955-1964	100	30.9	31.4	29.7	16.4	8.0
1965-1974	100	46.6	24.3	20.5	10.4	8.5
1975-1977	100	29.0	39.1	28.4	12.6	3.6

Source: *Flow of Funds Accounts, 1946-1975* (December 1976) for 1955-1973; *Flow of Funds Accounts, 4th Quarter 1977* (February 1978) for 1974-1977, tables on Credit Market Supply of Funds and Sector Statements of Saving and Investment.

Most financial intermediaries have no special need to hedge against the direct loss of their own purchasing power due to inflation, since their assets and liabilities are both denominated in fixed-dollar terms. For some, however, the difference in maturity structure of assets and liabilities—that is, the longer maturities of assets than of liabilities—creates a need to hedge against sudden increases in market yields which result from the acceleration of inflation. For all the intermediaries, the successive increases in market interest rates after the mid-1960s imposed real, if unrecognized, balance sheet losses and made them understandably fearful of further increases in interest rates. At such times of rising market yields, those that are saddled with assets of long maturity acquired at earlier low yields and with liabilities that are short term are subject to pressures to obtain the highest possible returns on new loans. Since all financial intermediaries naturally seek the best investment return they can reasonably obtain, changes in interest rates are relevant to all of them. The life insurance companies, which are relatively protected by the long maturity of their fixed-dollar commitments, aside from their obligation to make policy loans at fixed rates, are described (Lintner [1976]; and Lintner, Piper, and Fortune [1978]) as varying the rate of commitments for future loans partly according to expected changes in interest rates. In effect, the commitment rate depends upon expected future inflation rates, since these affect interest rates.

Equity features on loans were believed in the 1960s to reduce the danger of capital losses when inflation rates rose and pulled bond yields higher than had been anticipated. In the second half of the 1960s, as noted earlier, the intermediaries experimented with equity-type investments, in many cases on a much broader scale than had been customary. Their flirtation with equity-type investments can be viewed as a response to the uncertainty of accelerating inflation. An attitude took hold that an overly conservative investment strategy would miss opportunities for matching the performance of more adventurous competitors.

This attitude encouraged equity kickers and income participations, used in private placements mainly by life insurance companies. These were provisions for warrants or convertibility into common stock of corporate borrowers and, in loans to builders, a specified participation in any income of the project above a base amount.[22] Managers of many financial institutions became intensely conscious of rates of return and, in the tight money environment of the late 1960s, equity features held out the prospect of larger returns than could safely be extracted from borrowers by a high straight-interest payment. The subsequent outcome, however, was disappointing.[23] As prospects of bonanzas from equity faded and bond yields stabilized at a high level, the institutions returned to their traditional form of straight-interest lending.

Private pension funds are in different circumstances from those of deposit and insurance institutions. Most corporate pension funds have fixed-dollar obligations at distant future dates and discretion in funding. They receive contractual contributions from participants, who cannot easily withdraw. The corporate sponsors of these plans stand to gain from higher returns on assets. Nevertheless, as shown in Table 2-15, while funds increased their concentration in equity substantially until 1972, the concentration declined after that both because the market value of equity holdings fell and because the proportion of new funds channeled into equity was reduced in favor of government and corporate bonds. The shift into equities is somewhat understated because the totals for credit market instruments in Table 2-15 are in par values. If we estimate market values of long-term assets as we did market values of long-term corporate liabilities in Table 2-2, the share of equities would be about 65 percent in 1968-1970 and 75 percent at the peak in 1972. The share of credit market instruments would be around 30 percent in 1968-1970 and 36 percent in 1974.

The changes in the composition of net purchases show the shifts in direction even more strongly. The equity share rose from below 40 percent in the 1950s to over 100 percent, while the share of credit market instruments fell from 60 percent or so, and there were even net sales in 1971 and 1972. In three of the last four years, however, credit market instruments were again more than half of net acquisitions, even though equities still accounted for more than half of assets.

If equity had provided the hedge against inflation that the intermediaries were looking for, the public might also have found equity attractive and have channeled their savings into equity and not into the intermediaries. Then the intermediaries would have found a remedy to one problem only to face another. The disappointing performance of equity, however, precluded such a rechanneling, even assuming it would otherwise have occurred. Since they have weathered the storm of rising market rates several times during periods of tight money, there is growing confidence that intermediaries will weather storms of similar magnitude in the future. Although a renewed threat of increased inflation would resurrect the desire to find hedges, the unsatisfactory results with equity in recent years raise doubts that financial institutions would experiment with equity soon again in a replay of those conditions.

Government

Federal and local governments are major suppliers of securities and so can influence conditions in financial markets, as was suggested by the concern about "crowding out" of private borrowers in 1975. Inflation can affect government budgets and the supply of government securities, though the standard theory is not concerned with this sector and offers little guidance. Two propositions of the

Table 2-15.   Financial Assets and Net Purchases of Private Pension Funds, 1955-1977. (percentage distribution)

		Assets			Net Purchases		
	Total	Equity (market value)	Credit Market Instruments Plus Deposits (par value)	Other	Equity	Market Instruments and Deposits	Other
1955	100	33.2	63.1	3.7	32.0	60.5	7.5
1956	100	33.5	62.2	4.3	34.5	57.1	8.4
1957	100	32.0	63.8	4.2	37.3	60.0	2.7
1958	100	39.6	57.0	3.5	44.5	54.4	1.1
1959	100	42.6	54.0	3.4	47.6	48.4	4.0
1960	100	43.4	53.0	3.6	49.1	45.7	5.2
1961	100	49.5	47.3	3.2	57.3	40.3	2.4
1962	100	46.4	50.1	3.5	52.6	42.9	4.6
1963	100	50.3	46.5	3.2	51.0	46.9	2.1
1964	100	52.4	43.6	3.9	40.5	45.1	14.4
1965	100	55.3	40.8	3.9	57.7	36.1	6.2
1966	100	52.1	43.3	4.6	50.4	40.2	9.4
1967	100	57.2	38.1	4.7	69.5	19.6	10.8
1968	100	60.6	34.9	4.5	74.1	20.5	5.4
1969	100	60.0	35.4	4.6	84.9	13.0	2.1
1970	100	60.6	35.0	4.4	64.0	34.1	2.0
1971	100	67.9	28.4	3.7	122.9	−22.4	−0.5
1972	100	73.5	23.3	3.2	105.9	−8.2	2.3
1973	100	67.0	29.3	3.8	62.2	36.1	1.7
1974	100	54.3	41.2	4.5	21.1	77.6	1.2
1975	100	59.5	36.8	3.7	45.0	53.1	1.9
1976	100	62.5	34.2	3.3	57.5	40.9	1.6
1977	100	55.7	40.1	4.2	24.9	64.9	10.2
Averages							
1955-1964	100	42.2	54.1	3.6	44.6	50.1	5.2
1965-1974	100	60.8	35.0	4.2	73.4	24.7	4.1
1975-1977	100	59.2	37.0	3.7	42.5	53.0	4.6

Source: *Flow of Funds Accounts, 1946-1975* (December 1976) for 1955-1975; *Flow of Funds Accounts, 4th Quarter 1977* (February 1978) for 1976-1977, Private Pension Funds: tables on Financial Assets and Liabilities, and Saving and Investment. Insurance company pension funds are excluded.

standard theory of unanticipated inflation suggest, however, that government borrowing might decline under inflation. The real value of interest payments on outstanding securities would decline, and the progressive income tax would raise revenues in real terms. Also, a rise in nominal interest might run up against statutory limitations and prevent some states and municipalities from issuing long-term securities.[24]

Table 2-16 shows what has happened since 1965. Borrowing in real terms by state and local governments remained on a moderately rising trend except for a jump in 1971. Total real borrowing by the government sector rose substantially, though with considerable variation from year to year. The federal sector had large deficits, particularly in the 1970s, and federally sponsored agencies raised increasing amounts to finance their lending activities in various years beginning with 1969. As a consequence, the government sector increased its demands on financial markets and thus contributed to a rise in real interest rates, though some of these funds were returned as loans to nongovernmental sectors of the economy and thus were rechanneled rather than withdrawn from financial markets.

To what extent government borrowing was a response, and to what extent a contributor, to inflation is a complex question. No doubt it was both. In any event, from 1965 to 1974 (to exclude the unusually large 1975-1977 federal deficits), the increase in household financial saving of $79 billion (Table 2-12) was nearly half absorbed by the increase of $34 billion in borrowing by the government sector.

BEHAVIOR OF INTEREST RATES

The most dramatic effect of inflation in financial markets has been the extraordinary rise in interest rates (Figure 2-4). From around 4½ percent in 1964-1965, high grade corporate bond yields reached 8 percent in 1970 and have remained between 7 and 9 percent in the years since. High grade municipal bond yields rose from 3¼ percent in 1964 and 1965 to 6½ percent in 1970, and 5-7 percent since then. The Fisher effect implies such a rise. We can use these changes in interest rates to form a rough impression of changes in anticipated rates of inflation, assuming that there was no change in the real rate of interest. If we use the rate on corporate bonds, we would estimate that the anticipated rate of inflation over twenty to thirty years rose by about 4 percentage points between 1964-1965 (4½ percent) and 1975-1977 (8½ percent). If we use the rate on municipal bonds, we would estimate an increase of about 3 percentage points over ten to fifteen years, the usual life of municipal bonds. The existence of taxes on income distorts the estimates somewhat, presumably exaggerating the rise estimated from corporate bond rates and diminishing that estimated from municipal bond rates. Thus, if the early 1960s average inflation rate of 1¼ percent was also the anticipated rate at that time, expectations in the mid-1970s were for rates of inflation in the neighborhood of

Table 2-16. Net[a] Funds Raised in Credit Markets by the Government Sector 1965–1977. (billions of 1964 dollars)

| | Federal | | | | | | | |
	Public Debt	Agency Issues	Sponsored Credit Agencies and Mortgage Pool Issues	Less Federal Reserve Purchases of U.S. Government Securities	Less Other U.S. Government and Agency Purchases of U.S. Government Securities	State and Local	Total	Total in Current Dollars
1965	1.3	0.5	2.1	-3.6	-0.2	7.2	7.3	7.4
1966	2.2	1.2	5.3	-3.3	-2.1	5.4	8.7	9.1
1967	8.3	3.8	0.1	-4.5	0.1	7.3	15.1	16.2
1968	9.3	2.8	3.3	-3.4	0	8.5	20.5	23.0
1969	-1.1	-2.0	8.3	-3.6	1.6	8.4	11.6	13.7
1970	10.3	-0.8	7.8	-4.0	-0.8	9.0	21.5	26.9
1971	19.9	-0.8	4.5	-6.7	0.4	13.3	30.6	39.9
1972	10.6	0.6	6.2	-0.3	0.9	10.5	28.5	38.4
1973	5.5	0.3	13.9	-6.5	0	9.0	22.2	31.8
1974	7.6	-0.1	14.1	-3.3	-1.8	9.8	26.3	41.8
1975	49.5	-0.2	7.3	-4.8	-3.5	6.3	54.6	94.6
1976	37.7	-0.1	10.4	-5.5	-2.8	6.9	46.6	85.4
1977	29.6	-0.5	14.0	-3.7	-0.5	12.6	51.5	100.5

Source: *Flow of Funds Accounts, 1946–1975* (December 1976) for 1965–1967; *Flow of Funds Accounts, 4th Quarter 1977* (February 1978) for 1968–1977, tables on Sector Statements of Saving and Investment for Government, Federally Sponsored Credit Agencies and Mortgage Pools, Monetary Authority, and State and Local Governments—General Funds. Excludes state and local employee retirement funds.

Dollar figures deflated by annual CPI, all items.

[a] Acquisitions of government securities by federal agencies are deducted.

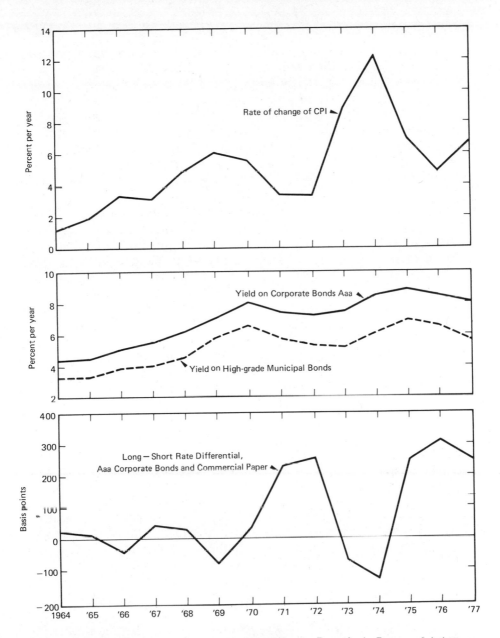

Source: Consumer price index, all items (December to December), Bureau of Labor Statistics. Aaa corporate bond yield (Moody's); prime commercial paper, four to six months; high-grade municipal bond yield (Standard and Poor's)—all from *Annual Report of the Council of Economic Advisers.*

Figure 2-4. Interest Rates and Inflation, 1964–1977

4 to 5 percent or a little more, somewhat below actual rates at the time, which were 6 to 7 percent.

Another question is raised by the rapidity with which interest rates responded to the rise in the rate of inflation, since past behavior suggested a long lag, attributable to the slowness with which anticipations come abreast of current developments. In his study of the earlier evidence, Sargent ([1973b], [1976]) found that the adjustment of interest rates to inflation had indeed been slow, but not necessarily because anticipations changed slowly. He showed that if anticipations of future inflation are simply extrapolations of past rates of inflation, as Fisher [1930] assumed, we should not expect the inflation premium in interest rates to completely compensate for the inflation rate in the short run. The reason for the failure to offset completely is that inflation is accompanied by increases in the money supply and decreases in the demand for money balances. Both of these produce short-run increases in the demand for various assets that offset to some extent the tendency of interest rates to rise in response to inflation. The result of ignoring these counter-effects on interest rates was to make the positive direct effect of inflationary expectations appear to be slow and incomplete. Using this theoretical analysis, Sargent was able to clarify the difficulties past research had encountered in testing the direct effect of inflation on interest rates. He concluded that the unreasonably long lags found for the effect of inflation on interest rates were due to this confounding of separate effects.

Yet it does not seem unlikely that before the 1930s or even World War II, long-term anticipations changed very little in response to current U.S. inflation rates, which were in any case generally mild. Because of the commitment to the gold standard, in which the long-run price level was tied to growth of the gold stock, prices would not be expected to stray far from a mild trend. Under those conditions, a sudden rapid rise in prices would be viewed as requiring a subsequent decline back to trend.[25] Although the complete floating of the dollar free of the gold tie did not occur until 1973, by the 1960s the public must have viewed prices as largely determined by nongold influences. Anticipations may have responded much more rapidly to an acceleration of inflation in the mid-1960s, therefore, than in earlier episodes.[26]

Even considering the likely reduction in the lag between price developments and price anticipations, the rise in interest rates when inflation accelerated in 1965 was extraordinarily rapid. As shown in Figure 2–4, bond yields rose year by year almost as fast as the inflation rate did. While the total rise in yields was a little smaller,

there is little discernible lag in the movements up to 1969. Other influences may have contributed to the coincident response. Business
demand for borrowed funds rose because inflation initially reduced
real internal funds for the various reasons discussed earlier. The
resulting increase in the demand for external funds did not depend
upon any anticipation of continuing inflation on the part of business
borrowers; therefore, it exerted an upward pull on the real rate of
interest. In addition, the restraint of monetary policies in 1966 and
1969 produced periods of financial tightness which also ran interest
rates up sharply, even though temporarily. These developments
alone could have accounted for much of the initial sharp rise in
interest rates in the second half of the 1960s.

Such developments do not explain the continuing high levels of
rates in the 1970s, however. To explain these high levels, we do
need the Fisher effect. Anticipations of higher inflation formed
and in due course maintained nominal rates at higher levels.[27]
However, anticipations of inflation may not have formed concurrently with the onset of inflation in the second half of the 1960s,
but may have been buttressed in their effect on interest rates by
the other developments mentioned to produce the appearance of
a rapid response of interest rates to each step-up in the rate of inflation (Figure 2-4).

It seems necessary to emphasize the increase in demand for funds
in explaining the initial rise in interest rates in the mid-1960s, because the evidence discussed earlier fails to show any reduction on
the supply side. Households did not reduce saving relative to income
or the fraction channeled into fixed-dollar assets. Apart from bidding
up the relative prices of residential property, households made little
shift into real assets. Any possibility of a constant or increasing
household interest in equity was dashed by the collapse of equity
values after 1968. Given that households continued to allocate an
increasing flow of saving into fixed-dollar investments, the sharp
rise in interest rates must have come from the demand side.

An unusual glimpse into the inner market workings of the Fisher
effect is afforded by the three month freeze on prices imposed suddenly in August 1971. Here was an "experiment" in suddenly
changing the anticipated rate of inflation. Few doubted that the
freeze would be enforced, that it would last the full three months,
or that it would successfully arrest the rise in most prices (only
farm products and a few other items were exempt) for at least
three months even if prices caught up afterwards. The price level
was in fact virtually frozen, and the anticipated change in prices
for the three months, August 15 to November 15, must have been

zero. Not much evasion through adulteration of the quality of goods could occur quickly. The nominal rate on three month instruments sold at the beginning of this period should therefore have fallen to the real rate, whereas just previously the nominal rate presumably incorporated an anticipated rate of inflation of 3 to 5 percent. What happened to the nominal rate when the freeze was announced? Instead of declining by the 3 to 5 percent, or 300–500 basis points, implied by the Fisher effect, it was little changed, declining in the week after announcement of the freeze by eight basis points for ninety-day prime bankers' acceptances and by forty-five basis points on new issues of three-month Treasury bills. (Over the subsequent four weeks, Treasury bills fell a maximum of eighty-three basis points, but this later decline cannot be attributed to the announcement of a three month price freeze. It would reflect expectations of developments after the period of the freeze.) Since short-term interest rates were around 5 percent during this period, a decline by the presumed rate of anticipated inflation of 3 to 5 percent would have reduced them to 0–2 percent. (Long-term rates depend upon long-run expectations and would not be expected to respond much to the freeze, as they did not.) What kept nominal three month rates from falling immediately and substantially upon the announcement of the freeze?[28]

One answer appears to be that the supply of short-term funds is, in any short period, virtually inelastic to changes in real interest rates. The only shift in a short period that in practice could reduce interest rates would involve money balances, but they are influenced by nominal—not real—rates. The price freeze had very little immediate effect on nominal rates, hence real rates rose; but households did not shift from variable-priced assets to bills and commercial paper on such short notice for so short a period. On the demand side, government and business were not in a position to reduce the demand for borrowed funds, despite the rise in real rates of interest during the freeze period. To be sure, if real rates rose and remained higher over a long period, firms would reduce inventory and trade credit financing, but clearly they would not make major adjustments for only three months.

Since changes in anticipations change market interest rates by shifting either supply or demand or both, the 1971 freeze indicates that the responses in demand and supply take time. Given the short-run inelasticity on the supply side, however, most of the adjustment to anticipated inflation probably reflects the demand for funds, and this does not change until business investment and financing plans can be changed.

It is certainly conceivable that, if a change in the anticipated rate of inflation is not viewed as temporary and if anticipations form rapidly, the response of interest rates could be rapid. This is the view of the new theory of "rational" expectations which challenges the older view that interest rates adjust to inflation gradually. The new theory holds that all available information on future prospects is used in forming anticipations of inflation. The implication is that anticipated rates of inflation are not extrapolations of past movements but are unbiased estimates of future developments. The errors over time may of course be sizable; "unbiased" means only that the errors tend to average zero. Extrapolations, by contrast, produce estimates biased downward in a period of rising inflation rates. Sargent ([1973a] and [1976]) showed that under rational expectations the negative effect on interest rates, mentioned earlier, would not interfere with the Fisher effect. An empirical study by Fama [1975] found that nominal interest rates since World War II exhibit no trace of bias in relation to actual inflation rates, such as would occur if anticipations were based on extrapolations of past inflation rates.

The new theory of rational expectations without bias is appealing. It implies not unreasonably (given the gains and losses at stake) that the public makes use of all available information, including sophisticated economic knowledge, to forecast market developments. It merits and is receiving further empirical testing. As for speed of response, however, it implies only that the public forms expectations as rapidly as pertinent information can be digested. This could occur slowly, since new developments are typically difficult to interpret until with time their permanence is revealed. It is therefore not inconsistent with the new theory of rational expectations to conclude that interest rates rose rapidly in the second half of the 1960s because of the effects of inflation on business finances and monetary policy and not because of a rapid adjustment of anticipations to the emerging inflation, though perhaps they formed more rapidly than ever before. That episode, therefore, cannot be taken as conclusive evidence that anticipations will respond to inflationary developments coincidentally or even very rapidly, though certainly they will sooner or later. It seems clear that anticipations do not change with every short-run swing in the inflation rate. The decline in inflation in 1975 and 1976 to 5-6 percent from the high rates of over 12 percent in 1973-1974 did not produce a comparable decline in long-term bond yields (which would have been over 500 basis points) to indicate a fall in anticipated rates of inflation. The obvious explanation is that yields had not previously adjusted upward to the 1973-1974 rates of inflation, because the public was not sure that the rate of inflation of those two years would be maintained over the next five to ten years. (It is true that short-term interest rates rose sharply in 1973–1974, but here the effects of monetary stringency and of higher anticipated inflation are difficult to disentangle.)

Yet there is no doubt that financial markets have become increasingly sensitive to prospective changes in the rate of inflation, as the public follows the latest data on prices, partly because of the consequences for monetary policy and interest rates. The important new development is that financial markets now *expect* interest rates to be sensitive to inflation prospects. This expected sensitivity, combined with the uncertainty about the rate of inflation, adds a new element of risk to long-term commitments. While investors may view current market yields as fully adjusted to current anticipations of inflation, there is risk of capital losses if the inflation rate subsequently rises above the anticipated rate. Such risk may account for a higher premium on long-term bond yields, as suggested by the puzzling and otherwise unexplained wide differential between high grade bond yields and short-term rates in 1971–1972 and 1975–1977 (see Figure 2–4.). To some extent, the differential could reflect anticipations of a long-run inflation rate which exceeds that for the period immediately ahead, but that seems unlikely because such a difference between long-run and short-run anticipated inflation rates would not prevail for so long a time.

The fear has often been expressed that financial institutions and markets as they have developed in the United States cannot survive in an inflationary environment. For the inflation rates so far experienced, this does not appear to be the case. To be sure, an important reason for the continued growth of fixed-dollar assets, despite their vulnerability to changes in inflation rates, is the absence of practical alternatives. Otherwise, it is hard to see how ceiling interest rates on savings deposits as low as 5½ to 6 percent can be maintained when the rate of inflation by any measure in 1976 and 1977 was around 6 percent or more and gives no indication of declining in the near future. Indeed, it is hard to see how zero real rates of interest can be maintained indefinitely. Interest rates will have to rise if inflation rates remain at present levels or go higher. Financial intermediaries will be under pressure to match such increases in payments to depositors, and, to do so, they will need some relaxation of current regulatory restraints.

NOTES

1. Securities and Exchange Commission, *Statistical Bulletin*, various issues.
2. Piper [1976], pp. 530 and 551.

3. "At their peak popularity in 1969, equity incentives (kickers) were included in approximately 35 percent of the debt issues that were placed directly with investors. This contrasts with a range of 0–10 percent during 1955–1967. By year end 1972, however, use of incentives had declined to a level only modestly above the average for the entire period 1955–1967, and it remained at a low level during 1973 and 1974." Piper and Arnold [1977], p. 278.

4. This behavior of manufacturing prices is discussed, with references to the literature, in Cagan [1974b].

5. A change in the real value of a capital good reflects either a change in the anticipated stream of real returns (as when a land site becomes more productive because of developments favorable to its location) or a change in the real cost of production of capital equipment which in the long run will induce a corresponding change in its marginal productivity, occurring through adjustments in the amount used relative to other factors of production. (The change in the stream of profits relative to the change in net worth will be consistent with the going rate of return on capital. The capital gain or loss to be recorded can be viewed as the discounted present value of the change in the stream of real returns to the capital good. It is implicitly assumed in making this adjustment of profits that depreciation schedules, in allowing for obsolescence, do not anticipate future changes in real value over the life of capital goods.)

6. Fabricant [1976]. See also Davidson, Stickney, and Weil [1976].

7. Shoven and Bulow [1976].

8. The larger part of the real capital gains recorded in column seven in 1968–1976 reflected increases in the real value of structures, owing mainly to the relative rise in construction costs. It may take time for the marginal productivity of these structures to increase commensurately through adjustments in the amount used in each industry (see note 5), and in the meantime, the increases in value may therefore overstate their contribution to the future stream of profits.

The accuracy of the price data used for measuring the real value of capital is frequently questioned. There is presumably some upward bias in the capital goods price index and, therefore, overstatement of capital gains due to the inadvertent inclusion of quality improvements in capital equipment as prices increase. Whatever the amount of this bias, it is not likely to have increased substantially over the period as a whole. Any overstatement of capital gains on this account is therefore fairly constant relative to the value of plant and equipment and would not be responsible for the wide swings in the value of this item. That is particularly clear in view of the fact that the adjustments in column seven were *negative* (indicating a decline in relative value) in the years of mild inflation from 1957 to 1964.

9. See Fabricant [1978].

10. The rate of return to net worth, which is an important determinant of the value of common stocks, is not appropriate for evaluating the return to capital. The latter is measured by the return to shareholders plus interest paid to bondholders as a ratio to the replacement cost of tangible capital. Some estimates in the literature of this rate of return to capital are reported in the Appendix. For this rate, the effect of inflation on the market value and real value of debt outstanding transfers income between stockholders and bondholders

and washes out. Capital gains or losses on tangible assets are also generally excluded.

The return to capital before or after tax has declined since the mid-1960s and in recent years was somewhat below its average level in the late 1950s. Its long-run trend has been variously interpreted as constant with a cyclical high point in 1965 and cyclical lows in the 1970s (Feldstein and Summers [1976]) or as upward until the mid-1960s and downward since then (Kopcke [1978]). The rates of return to net worth adjusted for inflation in Table 2-2 and Figure 2-1 show a similar though smaller long-run rise to the mid-1960s and decline thereafter. The rise and decline are smaller here mainly because the rising prices of the late 1950s and post-1965 years imposed real losses on bondholders which were transferred to stockholders. Whether such transfers continue in coming years depends upon the adjustment of interest rates to future rates of inflation.

11. This can be calculated from Table 2-3 as the ratio of the market value of equity per dollar of net worth at the end of the preceding year to current year after-tax profits per dollar of net worth at the end of the preceding year (Table 2-3, columns 4-8 divided by columns 9-11).

12. See "Recent Shifts in Corporate Financing Patterns," *Federal Reserve Bulletin*, September 1976, pp. 733-42.

13. Cagan [1974a]. Empirical studies of the decline in U.S. stock prices since the mid-1960s have appeared in increasing numbers. Nearly all of them focus on the negative effect of inflation on stock yields in the short run. A recent collection of these papers, with references to earlier studies, appears as "Session on Inflation and Stock Prices," *Journal of Finance*, May 1976, pp. 447-87. See also Fama and Schwert [1977].

14. See Lintner [1975], p. 275, for the theoretical reasons to expect this outcome. Also see Malkiel [1977].

15. Long-term market instruments are recorded in Table 2-6 at par values which do not reflect their decline in market price with the rise in market interest rates. Correction to allow for that depreciation would reduce the percentage share of this group in the years of rising yields. Since the percentage is low to begin with, however, the correction would make little difference to the share of deposits or equities. The largest corrections were from 8.0 to 5.9 in 1969 and from 10.6 to 8.3 in 1974.

It should be noted that household assets are estimated by deducting holdings by institutions from total outstandings. They are thus subject to errors in the totals and in any of the estimates of other sectors' holdings.

16. The household tangible assets counted here include only owner-occupied housing, land, and consumer durables. Tenant-occupied housing owned by individuals, and the associated land, are excluded. They presumably appear, with a deduction for mortgage debt, in other financial assets, as equity in unincorporated business. If they were included in household assets, they would increase the housing value by about one quarter in 1960. See Goldsmith and Lipsey [1963], vol. I, Table 70.

17. The estimate of the wealth effect in Taylor [1974], Table 8, is 3.4 percent.

18. Similar results for other countries are reported in Howard [1976].

19. See, for example, Silber [1970] and Kopcke [1977].

20. See also Deaton [1977]. A study by Springer [1977], however, finds that expected inflation does increase purchases of consumer durables.

21. Goldsmith and Lipsey [1963], vol. 1, ch. 8. The leverage ratio (L) is the ratio of the value of price-sensitive assets to net worth, price-sensitive assets being defined as tangible assets and common stock. The percentage change in net worth (W) is aL, where a is the change in prices of price-sensitive assets.

22. Piper [1976].

23. For a sample of sixty-five equity kicker loans negotiated during 1968–1969, Piper and Arnold [1977] followed the price of the stock and reported the following decline:

Mean Ratio of Market Price of Stock to
Exercise or Conversion Price

65 Equity Kicker Loans	*At the Date Exercised/Converted*	*At Year end 1974*	*On December 16, 1975*
17 Exercised	173%	46%	59%
48 Not Exercised	....	31%	34%

24. State and local governments were forced to cut back desired long-term borrowing by $5.2 billion from mid-1969 to mid-1970, a reduction of 28 percent. Petersen [1971].

25. See Klein [1975].

26. See Friedman and Schwartz [1976].

27. See Benjamin M. Friedman [1978a] and [1978b].

28. We are ignoring here the effect of international capital movements. If the exchange rate is expected to remain fixed (as it did for this three month period following the initial devaluation), U.S. and foreign nominal interest rates will tend to be equalized except for risk differentials and transactions costs. Since foreign interest rates did not change greatly, the equalization would have tended to keep U.S. rates from falling. But, in view of the incentive for U.S. investors and issuers to bid domestic nominal security yields down, given the zero inflation rate, the tendency toward international equality required a massive outflow of short-term capital. While there was a substantial capital outflow, it does not appear to have been sufficient to maintain U.S. rates at a level 3 to 5 percentage points higher than would have prevailed without the capital movements.

Chapter Three

Summary: Financial Adjustments to the Uncertainty of Inflation

Experience with inflation in the past decade has shattered many presuppositions. While it was once thought that the economy could follow an inflationary trend with no more and perhaps less fluctuation than in periods of stable prices, the actual course has been volatile for both the inflation rate and economic activity. Even aside from unusual years such as 1973–1974, when the inflation rate first doubled and then halved, the annual rate has changed by a couple of percentage points from one year to the next. These fluctuations affect interest rates and market values by a large amount. While it was once thought that inflation tends to reduce unemployment, the average rate of unemployment has been rising. In large part, the instability reflects the gyrations of aggregate demand policy, in which the economy is first restrained to reduce inflation and then stimulated to overcome the contractionary effects of the restraint. International disturbances add to the instability, as in 1973. But, in part, the instability also appears to reflect a change in the way that prices respond to disturbances in an inflationary environment, whereby market adjustments no longer moderate disturbances but tend to magnify them. So far, no new theory has been developed to explain and clarify the new behavior. In view of the difficulties of subduing inflation, no one knows when and if it will end, and adjusting to the possibility of continuing inflation is the prudent course. It was once thought that the economy would in time make all the necessary adjustments, but many of them are proving to be very difficult. They are taking a long time and may never be complete.

For financial institutions and markets, the effects of inflation have been extremely unsettling. (1) Interest rates have risen to high levels and undergone wide fluctuations, occasionally subjecting financial markets to disabling stringencies. (2) Common stocks have lost ground relative to the general price level and are subject to sharp declines whenever inflation speeds up or monetary policy takes steps to reduce it. (3) Long-term financing has become more difficult. The periods of the business cycle during which the market is receptive to issues of common stocks or long-term bonds have become shorter, and generally the public prefers short-term instruments to avoid the wide fluctuations in nominal value now associated with interest rate movements. (4) Households have not been attracted to common stocks as a hedge against inflation, and, although the total value of residential housing has risen, there has been no increase in net purchases of housing relative to disposable income. Although many influences were at work in the household demand for real property, a strong demand to hedge against inflation was not conspicuously a major one. Financial intermediaries did not find their short flirtation with equity kickers and income participations in the late 1960s successful and have abandoned them, although they have continued to invest in real estate on a wholly owned basis. One indication of shifts toward real assets is the recent dramatic rise in prices of diamonds and other such special items of wealth. Such items do not solve the problem of hedging against inflation for financial institutions and most investors, however. (5) Contrary to the presupposition that inflation causes a shift from fixed-dollar to real assets, household saving has increased largely in the form of financial assets, apparently as a response to the uncertainty of inflation. (6) Intermediaries have maintained their position in the financial structure, but they are vulnerable to short-run fluctuations in interest rates due to the variability of inflation and are severely buffeted whenever the rate of inflation steps up.

A central presupposition about inflation has been that financial markets would adjust to it and find ways to protect savers. While interest rates have risen to compensate for the anticipated rate of long-run inflation, common stocks, which were supposed to provide a hedge against the uncertainty of the inflation rate, have failed to do so over the past decade. The basic reasons are that profit rates have declined since the mid-1960s and that operating profits are subject to considerable fluctuation in an inflationary environment. Profit margins are squeezed by the tendency of costs to outstrip selling prices when inflationary pressures intensify and as frequent bouts of monetary restraint reduce demand and output. (Corporate profit rates in the aggregate recovered in recent years and reached the level of the mid-1960s, when measured by conventional dollar cost accounting. When adjusted for the effects of inflation, profit rates were lower in 1976–1977 than in the mid-1960s, though the level varies with the particular adjustments included.) The decline in profit rates and in their degree of stability led to a market revaluation of net worth from a high premium in the mid-1960s to a substantial discount in the mid-1970s.

If the low valuation of net worth in the mid-1970s were to be maintained or raised, common stocks would henceforth provide a positive real rate of return over the long run, even under continuing inflation. Even should the very long-term investor from now on be able to preserve his capital on the average by holding common stocks in an inflationary environment, such holdings will undergo substantial short-run fluctuations in real value with no certainty about the long-run outcome. Indeed, fluctuating rates of inflation make it extremely difficult to discern what sustainable profit rates have been and are likely to average in the future. The attraction of common stocks as a short-run hedge against inflation has for the present been radically reduced. Yet no alternative readily takes their place. Direct holdings of real assets such as commodities or property lack the ease of sale and management and possible diversification of investments provided by a portfolio of common stocks and are therefore not a satisfactory substitute. The inability of any available assets to serve as a practical hedge against inflation adds to the financial uncertainty of inflation and helps to explain the anomaly of higher saving in the form of short-term financial assets, which are subject to depreciation in real terms by inflation but which nevertheless are attractive because they do not undergo the large swings in real value of bonds and stocks. Contrary to the traditional view that investors should hold common stocks when inflation threatens, therefore, the recent experience indicates that both stocks and bonds decline when inflation escalates. At such times, cash or liquid assets have paradoxically appeared safest.

Present financial practices can hardly be said to offer satisfactory answers to the problems of inflation for short-term investors or reasonable safety to long-term investors. The bulk of financial assets held by households for contingencies and retirement are subject to uncertain rates of depreciation in real terms. Nominal interest rates on those assets may or may not adequately compensate for future inflation rates. In 1976–1977, nominal interest rates on many financial assets were lower than the rise in prices of 6 percent and gave a zero or negative real rate of return. The public faces the disconcerting prospect of accumulating financial wealth that may yield low or even negative real reaturns due to continual erosion by inflation. Furthermore, long-term financial commitments, such as home mortgages, harbor severe difficulties for borrowers in terms of their planned lifetime saving should long-run inflation rates decline appreciably and difficulties for lenders should inflation rates increase.

Financial practices seem bound to evolve through further attempts to provide a positive real rate of return and to adjust to the uncertainty of inflation. What direction such an evolution will take depends upon the severity of future inflation, changes in regulations, the success or failure of various experiments, and the response of the public. For example, present experiments with variable rate mortgages will undoubtedly continue, and their use is likely to expand if inflation continues at high and variable rates. Pressures to lift the prohibition of interest on demand deposits with commercial banks have intensified with the growth of checking privileges and phone transfers of interest-bearing deposits with thrift institutions, and the prohibition is not likely to survive many more years. Accounting practices to report business earnings in an inflationary environment are under review and bound to change, though progress so far has been slow.

These and other developments are peripheral, however, to the central problem of protecting financial assets against uncertain inflation rates. Securities linked in value to a price index, which have appeared in other countries, have yet to be introduced in the United States. Indexing is now a feature of social security and federal employee retirement benefits. The particular indexing schemes adopted were improperly devised and produced increases in nominal benefits that overcompensated for advances in the cost of living. The formula for indexing the benefits has been revised. The changes made may solve the immediate problem; but indexing is never perfect and other difficulties may come to light. Pension indexing in general presents the danger that growth in future financial obligations will outstrip growth in contributions and investment income and at some point require unplanned increases in contributions that are inequitable between younger working and older retired generations. Indexing of wages, which has a longer history, does not involve the same problem of making distant future commitments, because the terms are renegotiated every few years. But the present implicit indexing of many private pension plans, in which benefits are based on wages in the final years before retirement, raises problems about the current adequacy of funding.

The solution to the private pension problem would be the

availability of a diversified list of indexed bonds, but private corporations have avoided their issue, in part perhaps because of the uncertainty that the product prices of individual companies will rise commensurately with the general level of prices.[1] For the time being, financial arrangements are likely to remain subject to the vicissitudes of fixed dollar securities and common stocks. Additions to the present halfway measures to deal with the uncertainty of inflation await the financial innovations that current and future incentives for change can be expected to bring.

NOTES

1. One reason for such uncertainty is that the variability of changes in relative prices appears to rise as the overall rate of inflation increases. See Vining and Elwertowski [1976].

With its taxing power, the federal government could issue an indexed bond. Such a step would no doubt initiate radical changes in the private financial sector.

For one view on the future of private pensions, see Munnell [1978].

Survey of Adjustments of Corporate Accounts

Adjustments of corporate accounts for various effects of inflation give rise to a variety of possible measures of profits, profit rates, and ratios of market value of equity and debt to adjusted book value of assets. Several recent estimates for U.S. nonfinancial corporations in addition to our own are brought together in Table A-1 with an indication of the major adjustments for inflation that each one includes. Those of Shoven and Bulow [1976] are shown separately in Table A-2 because they did not calculate a rate of return, and their figures are therefore not comparable to those in Table A-1. None of the calculations go as far as ours in including all the adjustments listed,[1] but all include some or most of the major ones.

Some authors express the results as a rate of return on capital, and others, as we do, as a rate of return on net worth. The two concepts differ considerably in the level of the rates (the return on capital includes interest, that on net worth excludes it), but much less in general movements. The adjustments of financial assets and liabilities for inflation (items 2 and 3) affect the allocation of total returns on capital between bondholders and stockholders and are only applicable to the return on net worth. There are also differences among the sources in whether land is included in tangible capital and whether financial assets are treated as a resource contributing to profits. Minor differences exist owing to the use of different methods of estimating certain items and revisions in the basic data.

The market value of corporations including debt outstanding is compared with capital, and the market value of equity with net worth. The former has been denoted "q" by Tobin and is used to

Table A–1. Various Adjustments of Nonfarm Nonfinancial Corporate Accounts for Inflation.

Adjustment of N = numerator D = denominator	Profits plus Interest as Percentage of Tangible Capital			Profits as Percentage of Net Worth, After tax			Ratio of Market Value of Corporations to Replacement Cost			
	Before tax	After tax					Equity plus Debt / Tangible Capital		Equity / Net Worth	
	Feldstein and Summers	Holland and Myers	CEA	Malkiel and von Furstenberg	Kopcke[a]	Cagan and Lipsey	CEA	Ciccolo	Holland and Myers	Cagan and Lipsey
	(1)	(2)	(3)	(4)	(5)	(6)	(7)	(8)	(9)	(10)
1. Capital and inventories for change in replacement cost[b]	N,D	N,D	N,D	N,D	N,D	N,D	N,D	N,D	N,D	N,D
2. Market value of long-term debt for change in interest rates	not applicable			D	N,D	N,D		N	N,D	N,D
3. Real value of net financial liabilities for change in price level	not applicable			D	N,D	N,D	not applicable	N	N	D
4. Real value of tangible capital for change in relative prices				N	N	N	not applicable			
5. Value of land in D and change in relative value in N	D	N			N	N,D			D[c]	D
1955	12.4	11.0	6.5			11.4	.93	1.04	0.86	0.94
1956	10.6	8.3	5.8			13.0	.92	0.95	0.89	0.89
1957	9.8	5.4	4.9	4.8		6.3	.86	0.83	0.82	0.75
1958	8.5	4.3	3.8	3.9		4.4	.87	1.06	0.79	0.99
1959	10.7	5.7	4.9	5.0		7.2	1.05	1.20	1.01	1.00

Year											
1960	9.9	4.7	4.4	4.6		4.8	1.02	1.14	0.97	0.98
1961	9.8	4.9	4.3	4.3		3.3	1.15	1.44	1.13	1.19
1962	11.2	6.4	5.6	5.9		5.9	1.09	1.26	1.09	1.02
1963	11.9	6.7	6.1	6.2		7.7	1.20	1.46	1.22	1.14
1964	12.8	8.6	7.1	7.4	17.0	8.6	1.29	1.58	1.28	1.20
1965	13.7	10.0	8.1	7.9	18.0	11.5	1.36	1.68	1.37	1.26
1966	13.4	10.5	8.8	8.5	19.0	14.4	1.20	1.22	1.23	1.05
1967	11.9	8.8	7.7	7.4	14.0	12.0	1.21	1.36	1.22	1.20
1968	11.7	7.7	7.0	7.1	22.0	10.6	1.26	1.47	1.19	1.31
1969	10.2	6.1	6.3	5.8		14.4	1.13	1.21	1.13	1.04
1970	8.1	5.2	5.0	4.4	11.0	4.3	.91	1.00	0.84	0.99
1971	8.4	6.5	4.5	4.8	11.0	4.0	1.01	1.15	0.98	1.10
1972	9.2	7.8	6.2	5.5	13.0	9.0	1.09	1.25	1.04	1.16
1973	8.6	7.9	5.8	5.4	18.0	16.7	1.03	1.10	1.02	0.76
1974	6.4	4.4	9.9	3.6	18.0	16.0	0.76	0.73	0.94	0.42
1975	6.9	6.1	6.1	4.9	12.0	4.8	0.75	0.87	0.73	0.52
1976	7.9	3.5	5.8	5.1		0.6	0.84	1.03		0.62
1977			5.9			9.2	0.79	0.91		0.50

^aOn a current value basis. Kopcke also gives the decline in purchasing power of net financial liabilities, but it is not included in his figures for the rate of return.

^bThe adjustment for capital and inventories is the capital consumption adjustment and inventory valuation adjustment of the Department of Commerce.

^cIncludes the amount of cash on hand and accounts receivable and land at book value.

Sources: CEA, *Annual Report of the Council of Economic Advisers*, 1978, Table 8, p. 68; Feldstein and Summers [1977], Table 1, column 1; Holland and Myers [1977], Tables 7 and 2, respectively; Malkiel and von Furstenberg [1977], rates of return supplied by authors; Kopcke [1976], Table VI, column 8; Ciccolo [1978], data supplied by author; and Cagan and Lipsey, columns 8 and 11, Table 2–3.

Table A-2. Comparison of Shoven-Bulow and Cagan-Lipsey Estimates of Adjusted After-tax Profits.
(1964 dollars)

	Shoven and Bulow	Cagan and Lipsey	
		Excluding Capital Gains on Tangible Assets	Total
1955	25.0	24.0	34.9
1956	31.0	32.2	43.8
1957	18.7	20.8	23.1
1958	14.9	16.8	16.9
1959	27.6	29.3	27.9
1960	16.6	18.8	19.4
1961	18.2	19.3	13.2
1962	23.3	25.4	24.1
1963	28.2	31.1	32.2
1964	29.9	33.4	37.3
1965	41.6	44.5	51.3
1966	52.3	58.8	67.4
1967	41.6	48.8	60.3
1968	36.0	43.8	56.5
1969	50.0	60.8	78.9
1970	7.6	11.7	25.4
1971	7.5	9.8	23.8
1972	29.6	34.0	53.1
1973	58.3	61.3	103.0
1974	65.4	62.5	106.9

Source: Shoven and Bulow (1976), Table 7, p. 40, col. 11, deflated by CPI; and Cagan and Lipsey, Table 2-2. Total is column (12). Excluding capital gains on tangible assets is column (12) minus column (7) minus column (8).

measure the incentives for new investment.[2] The latter is used by us as an indication of the equity market's valuation of net worth.

The major adjustments listed in Table A-1 may be briefly described as follows:

1. Capital goods and inventories are valued at historical cost and therefore undervalued by conventional accounting procedures. The using up of inventories is usually calculated on the FIFO method, and an adjustment must be made to convert to the current cost of inventories used. Similarly, capital stock and depreciation must be revalued to convert to the current cost of replacement. The adjustments of the aggregate profits data by the Department of Commerce are used by all sources.

2. A rise in market interest rates, due to higher inflation or other reasons, reduces the market value of a company's long-term debt. This provides an immediate capital gain to corporations which have the use of borrowed funds at lower interest rates; the gain represents the discounted value of the saving due to lower interest costs on the funds until maturity of the loan compared with current market interest costs. Profits remaining for equity are higher, effecting a transfer from bondholders to stockholders.

3. The depreciation in real value of net financial liabilities due to inflation is a gain to corporations; it offsets any rise in nominal interest rates that occurs to compensate for the depreciation. If the offset is not exact, borrowers or lenders gain at the expense of the other.

4. If the current replacement cost of capital goods rises more or less than the general price level owing to changes in relative prices, the owners of existing capital are subject to capital gains or losses, reflecting the fact that their capital has a real market value higher or lower than they paid for it.

5. Similar capital gains or losses occur in the value of corporate land. To account for changes in the real value of land, it is of course necessary to include corporate holdings of land in the accounts, which only some of the sources do.

The major differences among the sources in the levels of the series can be attributed to the differences in definition, as noted. It was not possible without reconstructing the series to make them comparable in definition. The inclusion or exclusion of the various adjustments for inflation account not only for major differences in levels but in movements as well. Yet similarities remain: all the series show a peak in the middle 1960s, except for column (6), which has high values in 1973–1974 because of item 2; and all show quite low values in recent years.

The Shoven and Bulow [1976] figures, deflated by the CPI, are compared in Table A-2 with our total profit estimate and with our profit estimate excluding capital gains on land and other tangible assets except inventories. Shoven and Bulow would have included capital gains on land, structures, and equipment as a matter of principle but state that they omitted them because they did not trust the capital goods price indexes. While we would not endorse these indexes, we think the indicated rise in real land prices and relative decline in equipment prices for part of the period come closer to the truth than the assumption, implicit in Shoven and Bulow, that both prices moved with the general price index.

Among the other sources of discrepancies between our profit estimates and theirs are the use of different general price indexes; our inclusion of long-term bank debt among the liabilities, the value of which was affected by interest rate changes; their dividend adjustment mentioned earlier; and a different depreciation adjustment.

NOTES

1. An adjustment not listed and not given by any source in Table A-1 is that for dividends according to their real value at the time made during the year. This adjustment, given by Shoven and Bulow [1976], is small, however.

2. See Tobin [1963] and [1969]; Tobin and Brainard [1976]; and Ciccolo [1978].

Bibliography

Boskin, Michael J. 1976. "Taxation, Saving, and the Rate of Interest." *Journal of Political Economy* 86, no. 2 (April), pt. 2, pp. S3–S27.

Cagan, Phillip. 1972. *The Channels of Monetary Effects on Interest Rates.* New York: NBER.

* _____ . 1974a. "Common Stock Values and Inflation—The Historical Record of Many Countries." *National Bureau Reports,* Supplement 13, March.

_____ . 1974b. *The Hydra-Headed Monster, The Problem of Inflation.* Washington, D.C. American Enterprise Institute.

Cargill, Thomas F. 1969. "An Empirical Investigation of the Wage-Lag Hypothesis." *American Economic Review* LIX, no. 5 (December), pp. 806–16.

Ciccolo, John. J., Jr. 1978. "Money, Equity Values, and Income Tests for Exogeneity." *Journal of Money, Credit, and Banking* 10, no. 1 (February), pp. 46–64.

Conard, Joseph. 1964. "The Causes and Consequences of Inflation." In Commission on Money and Credit, *Inflation, Growth, and Employment,* Englewood Cliffs, N.J.: Prentice-Hall.

Davidson, Sidney; Clyde P. Stickney; and Roman L. Weil. 1976. *Inflation Accounting: A Guide for the Accountant and the Financial Analyst.* New York: McGraw-Hill.

Deaton, Angus. 1977. "Involuntary Saving through Unanticipated Inflation." *American Economic Review,* December, pp. 899–910.

Fabricant, Solomon. 1976. "Toward Rational Accounting in an Era of Unstable Money, 1936–1976." *National Bureau Report 16,* December.

_____ . 1978. "Accounting for Business Income under Inflation: Current Issues and Views in the United States," *Review of Income and Wealth.* March.

Fama, Eugene. 1975. "Short-Term Interest Rates as Predictors of Inflation." *American Economic Review* Vol. LXV, no. 3, (June), pp. 269–82.

*Paper entirely or partly a product of the NBER project on The Effects of Inflation on Financial Markets.

_____ and G. William Schwert. 1977. "Asset Returns and Inflation." Unpublished paper, March.

Feldstein, Martin. 1976. "Inflation, Taxes and the Rate of Interest: A Theoretical Analysis," *American Economic Review* 66, no. 5 (December), pp. 809-20.

_____ and Lawrence Summers. 1977. "Is the Rate of Profit Falling?" *Brookings Papers on Economic Activity*, 1, pp. 211-28.

Fisher, Irving. 1930. *The Theory of Interest.* New York: Macmillan.

Friedman, Benjamin M. 1978a. "Who Puts the Inflation Premium into Nominal Interest Rates?" NBER Working Paper 231, January.

_____. 1978b. "Price Inflation, Portfolio Choice and Nominal Interest Rates." NBER Working Paper 235, January.

Friedman, Milton, and Anna J. Schwartz. 1976. "From Gibson to Fisher." *Explorations in Economic Research.* 3, no. 2 (Spring), pp. 288-91.

Gandolfi, Arthur. 1976. "Taxation and the 'Fisher Effect'." *Journal of Finance* XXXI, no. 5 (December),pp. 1375-86.

Goldsmith, Raymond W., and Robert E. Lipsey. 1963. *Studies in the National Balance Sheet of the United States.* Princeton, N.J.: Princeton University Press, for the NBER.

Haberler, Gottfried. 1943. *Prosperity and Depression.* Geneva: League of Nations.

Holland, Daniel M., and Stewart C. Myers. 1977. "Trends in Corporate Profitability and Capital Costs." August. Processed.

Howard, David H. 1976. "Personal Saving Behavior in Five Major Industrial Countries." International Finance Discussion Paper No. 90, Board of Governors of the Federal Reserve System.

Kessel, Reuben A., and Arman A. Alchian. 1960. "The Meaning and Validity of the Inflation-Induced Lag of Wages Behind Prices." *American Economic Review.* L, no. 1 (March), pp. 43-66.

_____. 1962. "Effects of Inflation." *Journal of Political Economy* LXX, no. 6 (December), pp. 521-37.

Keynes, John Maynard. 1923. *A Tract on Monetary Reform.* London: Macmillan.

Klein, Benjamin. 1974. "Competitive Interest Payments on Bank Deposits and the Long-Run Demand for Money." *American Economic Review* LXIV, no. 6, (December), pp. 931-49.

_____ .1975. "Our New Monetary Standard: The Measurement and Effects of Price Uncertainty, 1880-1973." *Economic Inquiry,* December, pp. 461-84.

Kopcke, Richard W. 1976. "Current Accounting Practices and Proposals for Reform." *New England Economic Review,* Federal Reserve Bank of Boston, September-October, pp. 3-29.

_____ . 1977. "U.S. Household Sector Demand for Liquid Financial Assets, 1959-1970." *Journal of Monetary Economics,* October, pp. 409-41.

_____ 1978. "The Decline in Corporate Profitability," *New England Bank Review,* Federal Reserve Bank of Boston, May-June, pp. 36-60.

Lintner, John. 1969. "The Aggregation of Investors' Diverse Judgments and Preferences in Purely Competitive Security Markets." *Journal of Financial and Quantitative Analysis,* December, pp. 347-400.

*_____ . 1973. "Inflation and Common Stock Prices in a Cyclical Context." *53d Annual Report of the National Bureau of Economic Research*, September, pp. 23–36.

_____ . 1975. "Inflation and Security Returns." *Journal of Finance* XXX, no. 2, pp. 259–80.

*_____ . 1976, "Interest Rate Expectations and Optimal Forward Commitments for Institutional Investors." *Explorations in Economic Research*. 3, no. 4 (Fall), pp. 445–520.

*_____; Thomas R. Piper; and Peter Fortune. 1978. "Forward Commitment Decisions of Life Insurance Companies, for Investments in Bonds and Mortgages." *Explorations in Economic Research* 4, no. 5, forthcoming.

Logue, Dennis E., and Thomas D. Willett. 1976. "A Note on the Relation Between the Rate and Variability of Inflation." *Economica* 43 (May), pp. 151–158.

Malkiel, Burton. 1977. "Reports of the Death of Common Stocks are Exaggerated." *Fortune*, November, pp. 156–69.

_____ and George von Furstenberg. 1977. "Financial Analysis in an Inflationary Environment." *Journal of Finance* XXXII, no. 2 (May), pp. 575–88.

Moore, Geoffrey H. 1973. "New Work on Business Cycles." *53d Annual Report of the National Bureau of Economic Research*, September, pp. 14–22.

Munnell, Alma A. 1978. "Are Private Pensions Doomed?" *New England Bank Review* (Federal Reserve Bank of Boston), March-April, pp. 5–20.

Okun, Arthur M. 1971. "The Mirage of Steady Inflation." *Brookings Papers on Economic Activity*, 2, pp. 485–98.

Petersen, John E. 1971. "Response of State and Local Governments to Varying Credit Conditions." *Federal Reserve Bulletin*, March, pp. 109–32.

*Piper. Thomas R. 1976. "Income Participations on Mortgage Loans by Major Financial Institutions, 1966-1974." *Explorations in Economic Research* 3, no. 4 (Winter), pp. 521–63.

*_____ and Jaspar H. Arnold. 1977, "Warrants and Convertible Debt as Financing Vehicles in the Private Placement Markets." *Explorations in Economic Research*. 4, no. 2 (Spring), pp. 277–302.

*Sargent, Thomas J. 1973a. "Rational Expectations, the Real Rate of Interest, and the Natural Rate of Unemployment." *Brookings Papers on Economic Activity*, 2, pp. 429–72.

*_____ . 1973b, "Interest Rates and Prices in the Long Run." *Journal of Money, Credit, and Banking* V, no. 1, pt. II (February), pp. 385–449.

*_____ . 1973c, "The Fundamental Determinants of the Interest Rate: A Comment." *Review of Economics and Statistics* LV, no. 3 (August), pp. 391–93.

*_____ . 1976. "Interest Rates and Expected Inflation: A Selective Summary of Recent Research." *Explorations in Economic Research* 3, no. 3 (Summer), pp. 303–25.

*_____ and Neil Wallace. 1973. "Rational Expectations and the Dynamics of Hyperinflations." *International Economic Review* 14, no. 2 (June), p. 328–50.

*Paper entirely or partly a product of the NBER project on The Effects of Inflation on Financial Markets.

Shoven, John B., and Jeremy I. Bulow. 1975. "Inflation Accounting and Nonfinancial Corporate Profits: Physical Assets." *Brookings Papers on Economic Activity*, 3, pp. 557-98.

_____ . 1976. "Inflation Accounting and Nonfinancial Corporate Profits: Financial Assets and Liabilities." *Brookings Papers on Economic Activity*, 1, pp. 15-57.

Silber, William L. 1970. *Portfolio Behavior of Financial Institutions.* New York: Holt, Rinehart, and Winston.

Springer, William L. 1977. "Consumer Spending and the Rate of Inflation." *Review of Economics and Statistics* LIX, no. 3 (August), pp. 299-306.

*Taylor, Lester. 1974. "Price Expectations and Households' Demand for Financial Assets." *Explorations in Economic Research* 1, no. 2 (Fall), pp. 258-339.

Tobin, James. 1963. "An Essay on Principles of Debt Management." In Commission on Money and Credit, *Fiscal and Debt Management Policies.* Englewood Cliffs, N.J.: Prentice-Hall.

_____ . 1969. "A General Equilibrium Approach to Monetary Theory." *Journal of Money, Credit, and Banking* I, no. 1 (February), pp. 15-29.

_____ . 1977. "Asset Markets and the Cost of Capital" in Bela Balassa and Richard Nelson, Eds, *Economic Progress, Private Values*, and *Public Policy*, Amsterdam, North Holland.

Vining, Daniel R., Jr., and Thomas C. Elwertowski. 1976. "The Relationship between Relative Prices and the General Price Level." *American Economic Review* 66, no. 4 (September): 699-708.

*Wachtel, Paul. 1977, "Inflation, Uncertainty, and Saving Behavior." *Explorations in Economic Research* 4, no. 4 (Fall), pp. 558-78.

Wachter, Michael. 1976. "The Changing Cyclical Responsiveness of Wage Inflation." *Brookings Papers on Economic Activity*, 1, pp. 115-59.

Williams, John Burr. 1938. *The Theory of Investment Value.* Cambridge: Harvard University Press.

---

*Paper entirely or partly a product of the NBER project on The Effects of Inflation on Financial Markets.

Index

About the Authors

Phillip Cagan is professor of economics, Columbia University, and research associate at the National Bureau of Economic Research. His previous work in the monetary and financial area for the National Bureau includes *Determinants and Effects of Changes in the Money Stock 1875-1960*, "Changes in the Cyclical Behavior of Interest Rates" (Occasional Paper 100), *The Channels of Monetary Effects on Interest Rates*, and contributions to *Essays on Interest Rates*, vol. 1.

Robert E. Lipsey is professor of economics at Queens College, City University of New York, research associate at the National Bureau of Economic Research and director of the Bureau's New York office. He has been at various times Vice President-Research and Director of International and Financial Studies. Among his major studies for the National Bureau have been volumes on *Price and Quantity Trends in the Foreign Trade of the United States*, *Price Competitiveness in World Trade* (with I.B. Kravis), and in the financial area, *Studies in the National Balance Sheet of the United States* (with R. W. Goldsmith and Morris Mendelson).